THE INFORMATION SOCIETY

THE
INFORMATION
SOCIETY

WILLIAM J. MARTIN

Aslib

First published in 1988
by Aslib, the Association for Information Management
Information House
26–27 Boswell Street
London WC1N 3JZ

British Library Cataloguing in Publication Data
  Martin, William J. (William John), *1938–*
  The information society.
  1. Society. Effects of technological
  development in information systems
  I. Title
  303.4'83

  ISBN 0–85142–219–5

Phototypeset in 10/12 point Ehrhardt and printed and bound in
Great Britain by The Eastern Press Ltd, London and Reading

Contents

Tables

Abbreviations

ACARD	Advisory Council for Applied Research and Development (UK)
ADI	Agence de l'Informatique (France)
AI	Artificial intelligence
AT&T	American Telephone & Telegraph Company
BABT	British Approvals Board for Telecommunications
BLR&DD	British Library Research and Development Department
BOC	Bell Operating Company
BRS	Bibliographic Retrieval Services, Inc.
CAPRE	Coordinating Committee on Data Processing Activities (Brazil)
CCITT	International Telephone and Telegraph Consultative Committee
CDC	Control Data Corporation, Inc.
CET	Council for Educational Technology (UK)
CEPT	Conference of European Post & Telecommunications Administrations
CICI	Confederation of Information Communication Industries (UK)
CIDST	Committee for Information and Documentation in Science & Technology (EEC)
COCOM	Coordinating Committee on Export Controls (NATO)
CPE	Customer premises equipment
DBS	Direct broadcast satellite
DES	Department of Education and Science (England and Wales)
DTI	Department of Trade and Industry (Great Britain)
EEC	European Economic Community
EFT	Electronic funds transfer

EPROM	Erasable programmable read only memory
ESPRIT	European Strategic Research Programme for Information Technology
ESRC	Economic and Social Research Council (UK)
EURIPA	European Information Providers Association
FAST	Forecasting and Assessment in Science and Technology (EEC)
FCC	Federal Communications Commission (USA)
FDLIS	Future Development of Library and Information Services (UK)
FOI	Freedom of information
GATT	General Agreement on Tariffs and Trade
GDP	Gross domestic product
GNP	Gross national product
IBI	Intergovernmental Bureau of Informatics
IBM	International Business Machines, Inc.
IEEE	Institute of Electrical and Electronics Engineering (USA)
IFRB	International Frequency Registration Board
IIA	Information Industry Association (USA)
IIS	Integrated information supplier
IKBS	Intelligent knowledge-based systems
INTUG	International Telecommunications Users Group
ISDN	Integrated services digital network
ISO	International Standards Organisation
IT	Information technology
ITAP	Information Technology Advisory Panel (UK)
ITU	International Telecommunications Union
KDD	Kokusai Denshin Denwa (Japan)
LDC	Least developed country
LISC	Library and Information Services Council (UK)
MIDIST	Mission Interministerielle d'Information Scientifique et Technique (France)
MIS	Management information systems

MMI	Man–machine interface
MNC	Multinational corporation
NATIS	National Information Systems Programme (Unesco)
NATO	North Atlantic Treaty Organisation
NCLIS	National Commission on Libraries & Information Science (USA)
NIC	Newly industrialised country
NWICO	New World Information and Communication Order
OAL	Office of Arts and Libraries (UK)
OCR	Optical character recognition
ODD	Optical digital disk
OECD	Organisation for Economic Cooperation and Development
OfTel	Office of Telecommunications
OSI	Open systems interconnection
OVD	Optical videodisk
PGI	General Information Programme (Unesco)
PIS	Primary Information Sector
PSE	Packet Switching Exchange
PTT	Postal and telecommunications administration
RACE	Research in Advanced Communications in Europe
RAM	Random access memory
SDC	Systems Development Corporation, Inc.
SEI	Special Informatics Agency (Brazil)
SIS	Secondary Information Sector
SNA	System network architecture
SPIN	World Conference on Strategies and Policies for Information
SWIFT	Society for World Interbank Financial Transactions
TCC	Technical Change Centre (UK)
TNC	Transnational corporation
Unesco	United Nations Educational, Scientific and Cultural Organisation
UNISIST	World Science Information System (Unesco)

VDU	Visual display unit
VLSI	Very large-scale integration
WARC	World Administrative Radio Conference

Preface

The purpose of this book is to examine a series of social and economic developments which together have come to be known as the information society. Starting from an information science perspective it nevertheless attempts to place information in a much wider social context. This means that in this volume 'information' is interpreted in the widest possible sense, as reflects the interdisciplinary nature of the subject in hand. It is both product and process; a means to diverse ends, and an end in itself. Most important, however, is the projection of information as a phenomenon whose time has come, and whose interaction with social, cultural, economic and technological forces is producing changes of the order of those which occurred during the Industrial Revolution.

The book is the product of several years' study and teaching in the subject, both at Queen's University, Belfast and elsewhere. It seeks to put across a different way of looking at society and at contemporary events, particularly those in the socioeconomic sphere. It is intended for both undergraduate and graduate students in a wide range of disciplines or, indeed, for the general reader seeking to understand something about new technologies and their interaction with society. Although it is the sole responsibility of the author, it would not have been written without the help and encouragement of a band of people too numerous to mention individually, but all in some way connected with the Queen's University. I would also like to thank Peter Dale, who compiled the index.

Bill Martin
Queen's University, Belfast
August, 1987

CHAPTER 1

Information

Whether to the hunters and herdsmen of preindustrial times, or to latter-day captains of industry and commerce, information has always been important. Today, however, something is happening to information, to its role and status, its form and structure, that suggests developments of an entirely different order. Information has become a talisman, a symbol of political potency and economic prosperity. As a geopolitical phenomenon it carries implications for relations between nations, for the future of institutions, for value systems and for ways of life. Economically, information has already become a factor of such central importance that it is confidently forecast that the developed nations will be 'information economies' by the end of the present century.[1] While this chapter will focus directly on the subject of information, others will reinforce this general theme with a range of contexts – economic, technological, social and cultural. The overall aim is to consider the wider role of information in the modern world and, in particular, to look for evidence of the emergence of information societies.

What is information?

In a sense this is a question which anybody could answer. Information is all around us. Information is the staple diet of the readers of newspapers and the mass audiences of the broadcasting media and the cinema. It is directed ceaselessly at those millions of consumers so relentlessly targeted by the advertising industry, and is dispensed around the clock from any number of enquiry desks at railway stations and airports, libraries and similar public service institutions. In this popularly understood sense of the term, therefore, information is that which adds to our awareness or understanding of some topic, problem or event. It is variously perceived as facts, intelligence, data, news and knowledge.

This information can be delivered orally or it can come in visual form as data, text or graphics. To a considerable extent, moreover, the production and delivery of information is electronic in nature. In such cases, the end product is not just words on a page or even images on a visual display unit (VDU), but the outcome of remote sensing activities in outer space or of digitised transactions in the banking or airline industries.

Seen thus, information is an ingredient common to all areas of human endeavour, be they day-to-day affairs of business, matters of life and death, or the most trivial of pursuits. Without an uninterrupted flow of up-to-date and relevant information, governments could not govern, industry, commerce and the public services would cease to function, and the everyday duties of citizenship, from abiding by the law to exercising the franchise, would become impossible. Less seriously, people would be unable to gamble on horses, follow the fortunes of popular musicians in the 'hit parade' or consult their horoscopes in the newspapers.

Whether or not the recipients of this material ever give much thought to either its nature or significance is of less immediate importance than the fact that they require it and would be all too aware if, for whatever reason, it ceased to be available. In the circumstances, there can be little mystery about a concept which is of such obvious utility and importance. Surely the vast majority of people know about information and why it is important, if only to themselves? The difficulty is that there is another, more technical manifestation of the term 'information', and one which raises a number of issues of relevance to this chapter. These theoretical aspects, which include, for example, the interrelationships and differences between information, data and knowledge, will be considered below. In the meantime, let us look briefly at the generation of this everyday information resource, and at some of the uses to which it is put.

The generation of information

During the 1960s and 1970s the so-called 'information explosion' was the object of considerable attention, not least in information science circles. The outstanding example of the time was the exponential growth rate of scientific literature, reported to be doubling in volume every 15 years. However, little attention was paid to other, nonprint sources of information provision, such as the cinema and the broadcasting media. Today, with fears of information inundation if anything more acute, the focus of concern has broadened to include oral and electronic as well as print-based media. The information can come in the form of computer software, electronic mail, videotex or video, compact audio or optical digital disk and, of course, print on paper.

Somewhat ironically, that very information technology that promised so much in the way of controlling information output has, in some respects, succeeded merely in aggravating the problem. The onset of distributed information processing, with desktop access to word processing, printing and document delivery facilities, has undoubtedly swollen the volume of print communication, particularly as regards internal communication within organisations. It has also succeeded in a few short years in bringing into question patterns of information generation and communication built up over centuries, notably as concerns author–publisher relationships and the role and function of various information intermediaries in society. Not only is the generation of information something which occurs right across the social framework, but also the sources from which these various forms of information are provided and distributed have themselves multiplied. These range across a spectrum which stretches from the individual citizen or one-person firm at one end, to government and its agencies at the other, with in between an enormous mass of commercial and nonprofit information producers, distributors and coordinators.

This integration of functions need not necessarily mean the complete collapse of established practices nor the displacement of one social or occupational group by another. Hence, while in theory the potential exists for people to be their own publishers, the benefits of specialisation and the division of labour continue to obtain, particularly in relation to large volume, high-quality commercial operation. Similar commercial considerations have dictated the diversification of many traditional publishing companies into the field of electronic publishing. Nor, indeed, has the experience of information intermediaries turned out to be anything like that of the endangered species they were supposed to become with the advent of online database access. Although librarians and information scientists would be ill-advised to ignore the implications of direct end-user access to information, there are already indications that, far from being redundant, the intermediary will be in even greater demand in an advisory and interpretative capacity.[2]

There have of course been serious repercussions within the information community as a result of technological and other developments, and none more dramatic than the implications for information access and supply. Until comparatively recently, this would have been the clearly defined responsibility of certain established groups or intermediaries, including professional and voluntary bodies, government departments and relevant agencies. Furthermore, as a public service, this information would in the great majority of cases have been provided free of charge to the user. However, with the emergence of business opportunities in the provision of certain kinds of information, an additional class of intermediaries has appeared, whose relationship to the public is based not on ideals of service but on the pursuit of profit. Admittedly, a service is involved, but it is service at a price. This development has serious implications for the future of the traditional information intermediaries, for government information policies and the law of the land, and not least for information users. These and related matters are considered in greater detail in Chapter 6. This section, on popular perceptions of information, concludes with two brief examples of its application in everyday settings.

Information for what?

The areas chosen by way of illustration are education and entertainment, activities which at first glance might not appear to have very much in common. On closer examination, however, they will be seen to display considerable evidence of mutual reinforcement and support. This is apparent in an overlap in the communities served, in the complementary nature of their work, and in a shared interest in exploiting the potential of information technology.

Education

Information is the lifeblood of education. It is the essential ingredient in new ideas, in course content and curriculum development, and in the creation of materials and methods for teaching and learning. Therefore, the undoubted problems caused by an exponential growth in information of all kinds are more than offset by the benefits to educational development. The new technologies feature prominently in the production and dissemination of this educational information, and in its management and control. As a result, there has been a marked increase in the amount of informal learning, that is educational activity outside the classroom and involving students of all ages and levels of attainment. With not just television receivers but, increasingly, microcomputers and video recorders appearing in homes as well as in educational establishments, the nature and content of this informal education is also changing. Indeed, located as it is in both environments, information technology has dramatically altered the relationship between learning and leisure.[3]

Within the specific context of education, the major manifestations of technology are those of television and radio, with the use of microcomputers and, to a lesser extent, video recorders growing in importance. Although it will be some time before the full potential of even these relatively well-established technologies is realised, the advantages are already apparent and include: exposure to new ideas and experiences; development of logical thinking and reasoning abilities; support for training in new skills such as programming or for remedial activity in basic numeracy and literacy; and the simulation of real life situations.[4]

In informational terms, education can involve the use of television and radio for the delivery of software and access to 'courseware' written for specific subject areas. It can entail the use of microcomputers for access to viewdata and videotex, as well as to online databases. It can involve the use of a wide variety of interactive, multimedia learning packages, combining input from radio and television and from videodisks and cassettes with a wide range of published materials. Indeed, in the case of such programmes, the distinction between education and entertainment can be extremely hard to draw. Before turning to this entertainment component, however, a final word should be said about the general educational significance of information.

Already in schools, children are acquiring a measure of both computer awareness – that is, a general knowledge of computers – and computer literacy, which involves knowing how they work and how to program them.[5] The time could well be right for the development of these activities, through the provision of courses in what might be termed 'information literacy'. In this case, 'information literacy' denotes an awareness of the importance of information in everyday life, and a facility in obtaining, evaluating and using it for a wide range of workaday purposes. It seems not unreasonable to suggest that such understanding and its associated skills should be formally taught, rather than leaving to chance the acquisition of attributes deemed critical to future employment and life chances. This provision should be there for all who need it, for those in continuing education as well as those at primary or secondary level.

Entertainment

One of the most exciting developments in education in recent times has been a virtual revolution in the packaging and presentation of information. Subjects whose names were once bywords for boredom have taken on an entirely different aspect in the eyes of both teachers and learners. Much of the credit for these developments must go to the educational broadcasters, to people working within the major television networks, for example, or with the Open University. To pass muster at this level, programmes must not only be informative but they must also be interesting and entertaining. There can be little doubting the success of the broadcasters' efforts or the positive effects that these have had on the nature and format of the information subsequently provided. One result is that programmes produced for a specific educational purpose, and never intended to be anything other than minority viewing or listening, can quite unexpectedly generate demand at the level of the mass audience.

In the sphere of entertainment as such, moreover, there is a sizeable element of information content. Who has not by reading an historical novel or listening to 'drama-documentaries' on the radio acquired more than a smattering of information on any number of subjects? Surely it is as much the purpose of satire to illuminate and inform as it is to amuse and entertain?

Hence, throughout the entertainment industry, in the cinema, in the sports pages or the magazine sections of the newspapers, and even on radio music programmes hosted by popular disc jockeys there is a sizeable degree of information content, some of it more structured or scripted than others. Very little of this entertainment-based information would be available without a considerable amount of technical backup and support, much of it in the form of new electronic technologies. This ranges from the serious business of electronic news-gathering to the provision of videotex services offering cookery recipes, jokes, games and puzzles, even book reviews.

Therefore, information truly is all around us. It is a social constant, something that is to be found in the most unlikely and unexpected of settings. As was made clear at the outset, however, information is a concept that has two distinct and very different aspects – the popular and the technical. A fair amount of attention has been given to the first of these, with information treated in its everyday guise as news, fact or content. The time has now come to look in some detail at the alternative, more technical interpretation of the concept.

Information theory

Ironically, in this more objective and scientific approach to the concept, progress is bedevilled by the frequently contradictory nature of existing definitions, and by the absence of any consensus on the nature and characteristics of information. Hence, even the information science profession, whose interest lies in the study of information and related phenomena, is unable to agree upon an operational definition. Whereas progress has been made by adopting a conceptual rather than a definitional approach to information, thereby shifting the focus from the correctness or otherwise of the definitions to the usefulness of the concepts,[6] there are those who would question the value of either approach, maintaining that as information science is an empirical discipline it ought not to concern itself with the 'nature' of information or with questions of an ontological or metaphysical nature, which belong to the field of philosophy and not science.[7] Where the subject in question is the nature and purpose of information science, there may well be a point to such objections. In the context of a volume dealing with the role of information in society, however, they carry much less weight. Indeed, it is essential that some general understanding be established as to what is meant by information, in its formal scientific, as well as its more popular, connotation. This will be attempted by reviewing the perception of information within a number of disciplines.

The popular perception of information revolves around the meaning and content conveyed by the information transaction. Information is sought and provided on the assumption that the person receiving it will be better informed, whether this is in terms of the times of trains in and out of Paddington Station or the constitutional history of the United States. This concern with meaning and content is by no means confined to the general public, however, as the examples of the education and library services will confirm. A primary function of all education is the dissemination of information, while among public librarians the information function rests upon the content of reference, local history or community information files, that is to say, upon facts, data, opinion and even advice.

Among information scientists, the perceptual spectrum is wider, encompassing both the abstract and the particular: information is perceived as the written or spoken surrogate of knowledge,[8] and as the result of data processing, usually formal processing.[9] Wersig is not alone among information scientists in defining information as a reduction in uncertainty.[10] This approach is similar to that found in economics, where information is regarded as something which dispels uncertainty, for example in markets, in consumer preferences or in prices.[11] Unfortunately, in its efforts to come to grips with the fundamental concept of information, the information science profession has borrowed widely and not always wisely from other disciplines. Thus, coming to the study of information and knowledge towards the end of an illustrious career in economics, Machlup quickly disposed of certain long-held notions concerning the beneficial effects of information on both uncertainty and the decision-making process. He observed that more than 90 per cent of all information received is unrelated to any decisions or impending actions, while countless numbers of messages are received by people without any effect on their uncertainty.[12]

Although, in both cases, Machlup was using information in its everyday sense, the reservations about the link with uncertainty apply with equal force where more scientific formulations of information are employed. In one such instance Kochen, indeed, describes information as a reduction in uncertainty, but in the context of message transmission over a telecommunications channel, and involving such related concepts as entropy, order, energy, organisation and control.[13] Furthermore, Kochen was at pains to emphasise that, as used in this technical sense, information was completely divorced from meaning and the less precise forms of usage that could connect it to the kinds of information to be found in books and documents. These examples demonstrate not just the essential differences between the everyday and the technical concepts of information, but also the difficulties inherent in the wholesale transfer of concepts from one professional environment or academic discipline to another. In the conceptualisation of information, the outstanding example of this practice, and the major source of subsequent difficulty, has been the general appropriation and frequent misapplication of research findings in the field of communications engineering.

With hindsight it is hard to see how the problem could have arisen in the first place. The engineers went to considerable lengths to emphasise the essential differences between their perception of information and that which would give it any semantic connotations. Shannon's seminal publication was after all entitled 'The mathematical theory of communication'. Moreover, he warned that the term 'information' had a special sense and was not at all to be confused with meaning.[14] Indeed, as Machlup was later to explain, when engineers talk about information they are concerned not with content but with signal transmission. They do not mean the 'what' that is to be communicated but the instruction that the sender, by signals, conveys to the receiver commanding it – not him nor her but 'it' – to select a particular message from the given ensemble of possible messages. In this narrow technical sense of the term, therefore, information is the statistical probability of a sign or signal being selected from a given set of signs or signals.[15]

Nevertheless, the lure of scientific theory proved to be too strong for a generation of subsequent researchers, notably in the social sciences. It is hardly surprising that the resultant transfer of concepts and terminology devised for an entirely different, technical context was to lead to confusion over the very nature and essence of information. This confusion extended not only to the use of such obviously technical terms as 'noise' and 'entropy', which are considered in Chapter 2, but also to more familiar concepts such as data and knowledge, and their relationship to, and interaction with, information.

Data, information and knowledge

Few would dispute the existence of a relationship between data, information and knowledge, although there is unlikely to be unanimity as to its nature and significance. Data and information are frequently treated as equivalents, although there is also a tendency to regard data as unevaluated facts, as the raw material of information. Information, by extension, is data processed into some useful form. In his 'life cycle of a fact', Horton has traced the evolution of raw data from 'birth', into evaluated form as information, through maturity as knowledge, to 'death' and inclusion in the knowledge base.[16] Machlup, in describing data as anything that is given, no matter in what form or of what origin, nonetheless cautioned against overuse of the term 'raw data', in that even the most basic of numbers and statistics usually have to be produced by somebody, often at considerable cost. He also decided that the two were for all practical purposes equivalents, challenging the reader to decide whether information was a kind of data or data a type of information.[17] Like Machlup, Horton declined to translate conceptual differences into strict hierarchical form with, for example, information being seen as more important than data but less significant than knowledge. Instead he viewed each element as being uniquely important to the communication and decision-making process,[18] an approach which appears to have validity given that all three are marketable assets and, as will be seen in later chapters, potential sources of power and influence.

Among those who perceive such relationships in a more stratified form, Diener argues that data are sensory and perceptual phenomena, while information and knowledge are conceptual and, therefore, at the cognitive level of perception.[19] Likewise Jequier's four-stage 'pyramid of information levels', namely data, information, knowledge and intelligence, assumes that movement up the pyramid, from data at the base to intelligence at the apex, entails a qualitative, refining and evaluative process.[20] Jequier, nevertheless, is at pains to point out that his schematic is intended mainly as an aid to clarification and is not to be taken too literally. Used sensibly, however, such devices can be illuminating, not least with respect to the relationship between information and knowledge, two terms which will occur continually throughout the present volume.

The basic feature of this relationship is that the distinction between information and knowledge is much more marked than that between information and data. This distinction is valid for both the popular and the technical concepts of information, because there is no corresponding polarisation in regard to knowledge. Both in the everyday world and within the orbit of specialist theory and practice, knowledge is universally regarded as a much wider concept than information. It is a summation of many bits of information organised into some sort of coherent entity,[21] and the comprehension and understanding resulting from the acquisition of information.[22] Thus, to Machlup, information was a process, a flow of messages involving the act of telling or being told, and knowledge was a state or sense of knowing, an accumulated stock. He also observed that, whereas information and knowledge can mean the same thing, for example as that which is known and as the state of knowing, all knowledge is not necessarily information.[23]

Tedious though such distinctions might be, they are of more than mere semantic significance. In focussing on the narrower of the two closely related concepts, on information rather than on knowledge, this volume merely reflects what is actually happening in a world in which information is variously a resource and a commodity, the basis of individual decisions and national policies, and both essential ingredient and output of some of the most exciting technological developments of all time. Not that the importance of knowledge will in any way be underplayed, something which in any case it would be difficult to do given its close relationship with information and the importance of the knowledge base to the future development of society. Therefore, data, information and knowledge will be regarded as mutually sustaining elements, at times distinctly different, on occasions overlapping and interchangeable, in a common social process. This process, which for the moment can be termed 'the informatisation of society', to borrow Minc's phrase, will form the major focus of the book. In the first instance, however, what is needed is a perspective on information that conveys its essential characteristics as the hallmark of this new kind of society.

Information in perspective

In searching for such a perspective it can be decidedly off-putting to discover that just about every major authority on the subject seems either to disapprove of the concept of information or else to disagree with the uses to which it has been put. Thus, Fairthorne described information as being no more than a linguistic convenience that saves you the trouble of thinking what you are talking about,[24] while Wellisch agreed with Brouillon that any attempt at a scientifically sound statement on the nature of information should be abandoned at least until information scientists had reached agreement on some form of operational definition.[25] Just such a consensus in fact emerged from a symposium on information science held in 1965, where it was agreed that information was a 'category' word and that there are many kinds of information.[25] While true in itself this observation also helps to make the point that information means different things to different people. Much of the criticism of the concept, and of the uses to which it is put, has been in regard to the overexposure given to the mathematical theory of communication. Thus, Cherry regretted that the mathematical concepts originally stemming from Hartley should have been called information at all,[26] while Machlup deplored the condoned appropriation of a word for purposes that had not been intended by earlier users.[27]

For pragmatic reasons, there would seem to be merit in adhering to the dichotomy between the everyday and the technical interpretations of information. The popular version serves the needs of the great majority of people, and used in this fashion is perfectly valid. As regards the technical concept of information, while allowing for the particular circumstances of individual disciplines, it will be necessary to adopt a more coherent and realistic approach. To be credible, this perspective must recognise the proper context and limits of mathematical communication theory. It simply will not do to assume that a formula that measures physical signals will do similar service in the semantic sense in measuring the information content of written or spoken communication between human beings.

There is considerable potential in the approach adopted by Machlup, in which information is perceived as the act of informing or the delivery of a message and, therefore, is not to be confused with the object delivered – the content.[28] A similar argument was adopted by Buckland, to whom information represented not 'stuff', but the process of becoming informed.[29] This process also features in recent information science research, in which information is regarded as the structure of any text which is capable of changing the image structure of the recipient.[30] This is a complex argument, involving modifications to the conceptual structure of both the receiver and generator of the message, and further complicated by the notion of recipient-controlled communication.[30]

The purpose of such examples, however, is to convey a sense of information as that which effects some kind of change in a recipient or a situation. While reasonably compatible with more formal developments in information science research, this approach also provides a basis for understanding the overall role and function of information within society. In order to fully understand this role, however, it is first necessary to consider the contribution and influence of information technology. Why does information technology cause us to rethink the patterns?

The significance of information technology

The essential significance of information technology lies in its role as a change agent. It is a creator of possibilities, a truly enabling and liberating presence in our midst. No important field of human endeavour remains immune to its influence, no corner of life is left undisturbed by its coming. In the home, the telephone and television set have become gateways to an increasing variety of electronic services, many with a high information content. In supermarkets, point-of-sale terminals record transactions, update inventories and order replacement stock, often from automated warehouses and factories. Aircraft take off, cruise and land under computer rather than human guidance, while ticketing arrangements for everything from aircraft to hotel and theatre bookings depend upon the smooth functioning of automated systems. Although society is as yet neither cashless nor paperless, banking is now in many respects synonymous with electronic funds transfer, while electronic mail, word processing and desktop computing are ushering in the electronic office. This means not only faster, more efficient and cheaper ways of doing things, but also a completely different range of options.

Not that this is by any means the only possible perspective on information technology, as will become clear in succeeding chapters. Even in circles basically supportive of technological innovation and development, initiatives such as the British Alvey Programme on Advanced Information Technology were subsequently criticised for overemphasising the technological component at the expense of the real resource, namely information. This led directly to publication of the Information Technology Advisory Panel (ITAP) report on tradeable information.[31] Integral to such criticism is the argument that, for all its enabling characteristics, technology is basically a series of tools, and that, in overlooking this fact, people often confuse ends with means.

Not that the division between informational ends and technological means is in any way absolute. New technology is providing the ordinary citizen with a range of opportunities that go far beyond the technical sphere, and that promise new horizons in interpersonal communication and in individual and community development. Arguably, as people grow more accustomed to the benefits of information technology, they will come to be more appreciative of information, both as a system component and as an enabling force in its own right. For those who would question the use of such designations with something as vague and intangible as information there is a certain amount of prima facie evidence, not least that linking information supply to national economic performance.

Information in society

One of the most telling illustrations of the enabling qualities of information concerns the recent economic history of Japan. The so-called Japanese 'economic miracle' has been such as to strike both fear and admiration into the ranks of other industrial nations. In attempting to account for this success, moreover, a great deal has been made of certain factors, some of which have been more positive than others. Hence, there is Japanese industriousness and ingenuity. There is the contribution made by massive American economic aid in the aftermath of the Second World War. There are the benefits of a large and fiercely competitive domestic market, and of commercial protectionism at home and devious and unfair business practices abroad. To a greater or lesser degree, there may well be some substance in each of these attempted explanations, but this need not necessarily tell the whole story. Hence, whereas it is common knowledge that Japan is a world leader in computers and microelectronics, rather less is heard of its status as one of the great information-using nations of the world.

The Japanese preoccupation with the acquisition of information is long-standing and, in a sense, may help explain continuing criticism of its alleged commercial piracy and theft of industrial secrets. Of considerably more importance, however, is the fact that Japan was probably the first of the great industrial powers to appreciate the true importance of information and its potential contribution to economic growth and welfare. It comes as no great surprise to learn that it was Japanese scholars such as Masuda who first anticipated the emergence of a new kind of information-based society. Nor is it to be wondered at that a nation which places so much store by the acquisition, analysis and exploitation of information, a nation that more than 20 years ago devised a plan for the future computerisation of society, should now be setting the pace among the developed postindustrial economies of the world.

Clearly, economic development is a complex process and not one to lend itself to unicausal explanations. Nor, indeed, is any such explanation put forward here, the intention being merely to add a final practical dimension to this study of the information concept. As will by now be apparent, this in itself is a complex phenomenon, at once idea and entity, abstraction and commodity. In adopting an essentially open-ended approach to its task, this chapter has sought to shed new light on the information variable and on the nature of the society in which it exists.

References

1. Melody, William H., The context of change in the information profession, *Aslib Proceedings*, 38, 8, August 1986, 223–30.
2. See the articles by Sandra Ward in *Aslib Information*, 14, 11/12, November/December 1986, 260 and by Robert Mason in *Microcomputers for Information Mangement*, 3, 1, March 1986, 1–14.
3. Hawkridge, David, Progress in educational information technology, in *Handbook of information technology and office systems*, ed. Anthony E. Cawkell, Amsterdam, North Holland, 1986, 889–907.
4. Craig, Lynn, *This is IT and education*, London, Channel Four Television, 1984, 5–8.
5. Hawkridge, op. cit., 891.
6. Belkin, N.J., Information concepts for information science, *Journal of Documentation*, 34, 1, March 1978, 55–85.
7. Zunde, Pranas and John Gehl, Empirical foundations of information science, in *Annual Review of Information Science & Technology*, ed. M.E. Williams, White Plains, New York, Knowledge Industry Publications, vol. 14, 1979, 67–92.
8. Farradane, J., The nature of information, *Journal of Information Science*, 1, 1979, 13–17.
9. Hayes, M., Information science in librarianship, *Libri*, 19, 3, 1969, 216–36.
10. See Belkin, op. cit., 75.
11. Arrow, Kenneth J., The economics of information, in *The computer age: a twenty year view*, ed. Michael L. Dertouzous and Joel Moses, Cambridge, Massachusetts, MIT Press, 1979, 306–17.
12. Machlup, Fritz, Semantic quirks in the study of information, in *The study of*

information: interdisciplinary messages, ed. Fritz Machlup and Una Mansfield, New York, Wiley, 1983, 641–71.

13. Kochen, Manfred, Library science and information science: broad or narrow?, in Machlup and Mansfield, op. cit., 371–77.

14. Shannon, Claude E., A mathematical theory of communication, *Bell System Technical Journal*, 27, 1948, July, 379–423, October, 656–715.

15. Machlup, Fritz, Uses, value and benefits of knowledge, in *Key papers in the economics of information*, ed. Donald W. King et al., White Plains, New York, Knowledge Industry Publications, 1983, 245–65.

16. Horton, Forest W., Jr, *Information resource management: concept and cases*, Cleveland, Ohio, Association for Systems Management, 1979, 53.

17. Machlup, Semantic quirks, op. cit., 646.

18. Horton, op. cit., 61.

19. See Horton, op. cit., 54.

20. Jequier, Nicolas, Intelligence requirements and information management for developing countries, in *Information, economics and power: the North–South dimension*, ed. Rita Cruise O'Brien, London, Hodder & Stoughton, 1983, 122–40.

21. See Zunde and Gehl, op. cit., 71.

22. Horton, op. cit., 55.

23. Machlup, Semantic quirks, op. cit., 644.

24. See Wellisch, Hans, From information science to informatics, *Journal of Librarianship*, 4, 3, 1972, 157–87.

25. Wellisch, op. cit., 175.

26. Machlup, Fritz and Una Mansfield, Cultural diversity in the studies of information, in Machlup and Mansfield, op. cit., 3–56.

27. Machlup, Semantic quirks, op. cit., 642.

28. Machlup, Fritz, Uses, values, op. cit., 253.

29. Buckland, Michael K., *Library services in theory and context*, London, Pergamon Press, 1983, 95.

30. Belkin, op. cit., 79–81.

31. See Great Britain, Department of Trade and Industry, *Government response to the ITAP report on 'Making a business of information'*, London, HMSO, 1984, 10 pp.

CHAPTER 2

Communication

Communication is an essential element in this volume and, much more important, a key component of the information society. Information and communication are, for all practical purposes, inseparable, and in the strict technical sense of both terms communication would not be possible without information. However, for all its undoubted importance, the mathematical theory of communication has direct application to only one corner of a very large field. 'Communication' like 'information' is a 'category' word, there being many kinds of communication, in different subject fields and in different physical forms. As is the case with information, therefore, the operational context can be very important. While not concentrating on any particular subject context, such as linguistic or educational communication, this chapter will seek to establish a general awareness of human communication, a process based upon highly developed learning facilities, on language, and on social organisation.

What is communication?

In the popularly understood sense of the term, 'communication' can mean anything from the exchange of news or information between two friends in face-to-face conversation, to the transmission of live television broadcasts via communications satellites. In more formal circumstances it has been defined as the mechanism by which all human relations exist and develop; all the symbols of the mind together with the means of conveying them through space and preserving them in time.[1] Narrowing this formal approach somewhat, communication has also been described as the transfer of meaning[2] and, again, as the discriminatory response of an organisation to a stimulus.[3] Although perfectly valid so far as they go, neither of these two versions will serve adequately as general descriptions. In the first place, the term 'communication' has been in use for centuries without any connotation of the transmission of ideas or meanings from a source to a recipient.[4] In the second place, it is necessary to specify the stimulus concerned, to distinguish between human language and the communicative signs of animals.[5] It was thus that

15

Cherry described man as a 'communicating animal' and defined communication as the establishment of a social unit from the use of language or signs; the sharing of common sets of rules for various goal-seeking activities.[6]

Cherry's approach has several advantages, not least the fact that it has the potential of broad applicability. Even more important for present purposes is its emphasis upon the social nature of communication. The entire universe of human relations can be portrayed in terms of a vast array of communication, involving nations and individuals, organisations and institutions in an endless process. Whatever the type or form of this communication, it can be regarded as a series of exchanges involving the sharing of experience or the attempt to learn from, or to exert influence on, the opinions or behaviour of others. These exchanges can be in written, oral or tactile form. They can take expression as a letter to a friend or a business telephone call, as a handshake or a pat on the back. They can also find expression as nonverbal communication or 'body language', for example the use of gestures or facial expressions, or through adherence or not to established social codes of dress or conduct. Critically, however, they comprise processes of communication in an inherently related social context.

The communication process

Communication is not something that happens in a disjointed 'stop-start' fashion. It is an endless and continuing process in which everybody is involved. Furthermore, it is a process the operation and principles of which can be applied to a wide range of social situations. This has resulted not only in the widespread use of linear models of communication, but also in a common terminology, with, for example, terms such as 'channel' or 'noise', which originated in an engineering context, being capable of wide general use. The problems inherent in an overuse of such concepts will be considered below, but first let us examine the classic communication process.

The communication process requires at least three elements: source, message and destination. Known also as the sender or the initiator, the source is the point at which messages originate. It can be an individual or an organisation, a human being or a machine. The message may be in audible, visual or tactile form, as any signal capable of meaningful interpretation. The destination or recipient, which again can be a person or a group of persons, is the final link in the communication chain, the intended target of the message. The basic linear model of communication is therefore:

source – message – destination

Schramm described this process as one of establishing a 'commonness' between receiver and sender, or getting them 'tuned' together for a particular message.[7] For this to happen in practice, two conditions need to be satisfied. First the messages must be encoded at source into a form suitable for transmission and for subsequent decoding by the intended recipients. Second, in order for these messages to be equally meaningful to both parties, sender and recipient must share some common basis of experience in, say, language or concepts, in ways of looking at the world.[7] This commonality of experience is exploited by particular combinations of signs chosen by the sender to evoke the required response from the recipient. The process of communication, therefore, is one of transmission and reception, the passing of ideas, information and attitudes from person-to-person.[8] What then of the elements in this process?

The elements of communication

All communication operates on the basis of signs, the study of which is known as semiotics. The essential importance of these signs lies in what they represent, rather than in what they are in themselves.[9] These representations include human and other languages, such as morse or semaphore codes and the binary language of computing. In addition to the broad division between the human language of writing and speech and those languages employed in machine or other formalised rule systems, there are the concepts of object language and meta language, the use of which helps the student of communication to distinguish between the phenomenon itself and a description of that phenomenon. Thus, in the case of a conversation between two people, object language is the actual conversation or event, and meta language the language used by an observer in describing that event.[10] Therefore, language is a form of symbolism, with the symbols or, in human speech, words serving as empirical signs for the things they represent.

Signs are the elementary carriers of meaning and information, the means by which all communication takes place. They can be defined as transmissions or constructs by which one organism affects the behaviour or state of another in a communication situation.[11] The nine elementary types of sign find expression in every shape and form, from words and numbers to gestures and emblems, and every sign has three basic structural dimensions: syntactic, semantic and pragmatic. All three dimensions concern signs and relations, that is rules for a language which, abstracted from real life for purposes of study, are set out in meta language. The pragmatic dimension is concerned with the study of signs in relation to users, and as such it bears most resemblance to real life. The semantics dimension is concerned with relations between signs and their designata (those things which are referred to) and is more artificial in nature.

Syntactics is abstracted still further from the real-life situation and is concerned with relations between signs.[12]

In focussing on the symbols that human beings use in order to convey meanings, semiotics has provided a powerful apparatus for the study of communication. Here, 'meaning' is used in the sense employed by Cherry, with a careful distinction drawn between the intended meaning of the sender of a message and that interpreted by the receiver.[13] A message is an ordered selection from an agreed set of signs intended to communicate information, and is to be distinguished from a signal, which is the physical embodiment of the message.[14] Signals do not convey information as such, but have information content through their selection potential. Signals provide the means of discriminating between, and selecting from, various alternatives facing the recipient, for example a set of signs in an alphabet. Provided this alphabet is specified and is the same for both sender and receiver, the source can select signs from it, assemble them into messages and send them as signals to their destination.[15]

Finally, it is important to mention the role played by redundancy in combatting the ambiguities and uncertainties of the communications environment. Redundancy entails the inclusion in a message of more information than is strictly necessary in order to reduce the possibility of misunderstanding at the receiving end of the channel. It is a concept which applies on two levels: the semantic and the syntactic. Semantic redundancy involves an expansion of phrases and sentences until the sender is satisfied that the meaning of the message will be conveyed. This in turn leads to an increase in signs, that is in syntactic redundancy.[16]

Two perspectives on communication

Redundancy in communication is necessary owing to the presence of 'noise'. All communication signals are subject to this unwanted disturbance or interference, which is not part of the signal but can cause it to break-up or otherwise degrade it. As has been intimated earlier in this chapter, concepts such as noise have been adopted in other fields and particularly by researchers interested in the human aspects of communication. Unfortunately, these are essentially mathematical concepts, for use under clearly defined conditions, and their casual application elsewhere can cause problems. In view of the importance of this underlying theory, its implications for the general processes of communication will be briefly reviewed. This will be balanced by an overview of the broader social manifestations of the communication process.

The wider implications of mathematical communication theory

This theory is concerned with a mathematical representation of the conditions and parameters affecting the transmission and processing of information. Its unique feature is the use of a numerical measure of the amount of information gained when the contents of a message are learned. Hartley laid much of the groundwork for communication theory during the 1920s in comparative assessments of the capacity of telecommunications systems. These efforts were brought to fruition in 1948–49 by Shannon's work on the Capacity Theorem, which, by providing a measure for information, solved the critical problem of finding a definition for signalling rate. As a result the mathematical characterisation of the communication process has revealed a number of very important features, including the rate at which information is produced at source, the capacity of the channel for handling information, and the average amount of information contained in a message of any particular type.[17]

The fact that these aspects of the communication process are both definable and measurable has resulted in their application to the study of distinctly different situations and problems within the social sciences, for instance to matters of social stratification and community.[18] Nevertheless, the information which features in the mathematical theory of communication is of a distinctive and specialised type. As Fairthorne observed, the communications engineer has a very narrow semantics, which refers only to the statistical properties of the language of the message and not to its sense or seemliness.[19] As a theory, it lies at the syntactic level of sign theory, which involves rules of syntax and relations between signs, and is abstracted from both the semantic and pragmatic levels, which, as we have seen, deal respectively with relations between signs and designata and between signs and their users.[20] Hence, while a necessary condition to the understanding of human communication, the mathematical theory is by no means sufficient in itself.

The social aspects of communication

Few have demonstrated more clearly than Cherry the nature of the relationship between the mathematical theory and general theories of communication. Nonetheless, running through his standard work on the subject is the clearest possible recognition of the essentially social characteristics of the communication process. Hence, while attesting to our ever-growing dependence upon the technical means of communication, he reiterates the social function and purpose of telecommunications, the sharing and associating that marks man off as a social creature.[20] This can mean the sharing not just of communication space by the exchange of news, opinion or knowledge, but, indeed, of living space, by associating in communities, organisations and institutions. Furthermore, be these businesses, industries or armies, they have a formal structure and rules, which determine patterns of communication and how these can unite the various elements of the organisation into one purposeful, goal-seeking organism.[21]

For all practical purposes, communication and organisation are corollaries, the existence of one signifying the presence of the other. In the case of business organisations, with complaints about poor communication a virtual fact of life, it is a matter of fundamental importance, irrespective of the nature or size of the company concerned.[22] In more general terms, communication is perhaps *the* quintessential human activity, and individual instances must be perceived and analysed in relation to their particular context, and according to a range of potential environments: social, economic, political, cultural and technological. In the final analysis, moreover, the determining factor will be the human one, and this irrespective of whether the communication involved takes place across the garden fence, within the cut and thrust of business or, indeed, in the world of international politics.[23]

Communication at the individual and the mass level

While obvious, this assertion of the primacy of the human element in communication will bear restatement. This basic human characteristic is not to be explained in terms of communications technology or of its application to specific social situations. Although understanding can be enhanced in this fashion, to concentrate upon the 'means' of communication at the expense of the 'ends' towards which it is being used would be to overlook its truly social nature and purpose. This purpose has been ably restated by a number of 'religious-existentialist' philosophers, who assert that communication is the universal condition of man's being. In their view, existence is communication and life a dialogue maintained by human contact and a continual search for common ground.[24] In calling for a 'counter-revolution of dialogue', to redress the balance away from a situation of growing social control and alienation through cybernetics and the mass media, towards one which is more favourable to humanity, these philosophers have brought a fresh perspective to the study of communication.

In such studies, moreover, a concern with the role and influence of mass communication has been by no means confined to the rarified altitudes of philosophical discourse. This is hardly surprising given the sheer scale of the mass media and the fact that they play such an important part in modern life, as the purveyors of news, information, entertainment and, indeed, values. Whether at the mass or the interpersonal level, the same basic elements of source, channel and destination are present in the communication process. In mass communication, however, the relationship between source and destination is decidedly different from that which obtains in a situation of individual or interpersonal communication. Essentially, this is a matter of the 'one-to-one' exchange which obtains in interpersonal communication, as contrasted with the 'one-to-many' experience of mass communications, where a few sources transmit to a vast number of destinations.

A second area of difference arises from the fact that, unlike the face-to-face situation of interpersonal communication, mass communication is a mediated affair. This means that in mass communication, feedback can only be indirect and, where it happens, it occurs after an interval rather than simultaneously as in face-to-face contact. Nevertheless, there is feedback in mass communication, which, as de Sola Pool observed, is both anticipated and actual. Hence, not only do journalists anticipate all kinds of feedback from their audiences, but also if a journal or a television programme runs a particularly controversial item then the audience will let it know.[23]

Obviously, people communicate for effect and we have seen that unless some behavioural or attitudinal change occurs in the recipient no communication is deemed to have taken place. The bulk of concern with the effects of the mass media is that they will somehow condition their audiences to a particular view of life, or that in specific instances, such as with very young television viewers, they will encourage antisocial or deviant behaviour. Although it would be foolish to dismiss such reservations out-of-hand, it has to be said that, so far as the actual mechanisms are concerned, it is still far from clear exactly why some forms of communication succeed in their objectives and others do not.

According to Schramm, only two things can be said with confidence about the likely effects of communication. These are that a message is more likely to succeed if it fits into the goal, attitude and value systems of the intended recipient; and that of the various forces determining the outcome, only one is under the control of the communicator, and that is the message itself.[25] So far as mass communications are concerned, moreover, we cannot predict the effects of any communication upon the mass audience, but only on individuals within these audiences.

Conclusion

In an open society, it is clearly in the common interest that such important public institutions as the mass media function to best effect. Indeed, with the kind of personalised, truly interactive media now becoming a realistic possibility because of the new information technologies, there is the prospect of greatly enhanced public and private communications networking together to provide hitherto undreamed of facilities. The extent, if any, to which this potential is realised depends very much upon the human factor. It is upon such considerations as individual and group norms and values, private and corporate interests, the desire and ability to communicate, willingness to share, to listen and to see the other person's point of view – it is upon such considerations that the communication process and its development stands or falls.

Finally, it requires no great effort of the imagination to realise that in the world of today what is important for communication is by and large of equal importance to society. Presumably, it was in this spirit that the existentialist theory of communication was portrayed as a theory of knowledge?[26] Although attractive from the viewpoint of current interest in an information society, it matters little whether this statement holds water or not. In the final analysis, information, communication and society will continue to be critically intertwined elements of fundamental importance to all societies, however these are designated.

References

1. Schramm, Wilbur, How communication works, in *Mass communications: selected readings for librarians*, ed. K.J. McGarry, London, Bingley, 1972, 17–38.
2. Faibisoff, Sykvia G. and Donald P. Ely, Information and information needs, in *Key papers in the design and evaluation of information systems*, D.W. King, White Plains, New York, Knowledge Industry Publications, 1978, 270–89.
3. Stevens, S.S., Introduction: a definition of communication, *Journal of the Acoustical Society of America*, 22, 6, November 1950, 689–90.
4. Machlup, Fritz and Una Mansfield, Cultural diversity in studies of information, in *The study of information: interdisciplinary messages*, ed. Fritz Machlup and Una Mansfield, New York, Wiley, 1983, 3–56.
5. Cherry, Colin, *On human communication: a review, a survey and a criticism*, Cambridge, Massachusetts, MIT Press, 1957, 7.
6. Ibid., 303 (Appendix).
7. Schramm, op. cit., 20–22.
8. Williams, Raymond, *Communications*, London, Chatto & Windus, 1966, 17.
9. Laferriere, Daniel, Making room for semiotics, *Academe*, 65, November 1979, 434–40.
10. Cherry, op. cit., 11.
11. Ibid., 306 (Appendix).
12. Ibid., 221.
13. Ibid., 114.
14. Ibid., 305–6.
15. Ibid., 109.
16. Ibid., 117.
17. *Encyclopedia Britannica*, 15th edn, vol. 6, Chicago, Britannica, 1985, 312.

18. Pool, Ithiel de Sola et al., *Handbook of communication*, Chicago, Rand McNally, 1973, 19.
19. Fairborne, R.A., The theory of communication, *Aslib Proceedings*, 6, 4, November 1954, 255–67.
20. Cherry, op. cit., 9.
21. Ibid., 22.
22. Porter, Lyman et al., *Behaviour in organisations*, New York, McGraw Hill, 1984, 95.
23. Pool, op. cit., 19.
24. Matson, Floyd and Ashley Montague, eds., *The human dialogue: perspectives on communication*, New York, Free Press, 1967, 5–6.
25. Schramm, op. cit., 38.
26. Matson and Montague, op. cit., 6.

CHAPTER 3

Information technology

As a concept, information technology exerts universal appeal in the world of today. Identified in many countries as perhaps the single most important means to the attainment of economic, social and political ends, it has also become an issue, the focus of debate and contention. This chapter seeks to introduce the major trends in the development of information technology and to consider some of their wider implications.

Not surprisingly for a term of such widespread currency, information technology is something of a moveable feast, a shifting complex of meanings and interpretations. At once the most mundane of domestic appliances and the latest marvels of space travel, information technology spans a definitional spectrum that includes microprocessors, cable access television, fibre optics, satellites, teletext, word processing, electronic mail, video, robotics and much more.

This diversity has been captured quite effectively in a Department of Trade and Industry definition of information technology, which encompasses information use and content as well as the technology itself:

> Information technology is the acquisition, processing, storage, dissemination and use of vocal, pictorial, textual and numerical information by a microelectronics-based combination of computing and telecommunications.[1]

Enabling technologies

Broad though it is in concept and application, information technology is essentially the product of advances in the three key areas of computing, telecommunications and microelectronics. Indeed, such is their impact and significance that these are widely regarded as 'enabling technologies', the facilitators of change and the creators of hitherto unimaginable possibilities. Their overall effect upon society has been little short of revolutionary.

Computers

Although computers are simply assemblages of electronic and other devices that perform prescribed operations on coded data, for many people today they epitomise the highest level of technological advancement. Indeed, in a wider sense they have come to symbolise the age in which we live. Whether it is 'big bang' in the City of London, the replacement of humans by robots on the factory floor, or the guidance systems for intercontinental ballistic missiles, computers are a pervasive and inescapable presence. Indeed, with desktop computers established in homes as well as in offices, this diffusion of information technology can truly be described as an event of major social significance.

Such has been the advance of computing technology that in barely 50 years the computer has gone through four generations of development, each one more sophisticated than the last. Today the race is on to develop the fifth-generation computer, which on present indications will be a 'shell' enclosing such features as expert systems, intelligent knowledge-based systems and knowledge engineering, and facilitating unprecedented advances in processing power and human–computer interaction. Computing received a considerable boost during the 1950s when vacuum tubes were replaced by transistors, and when entire assemblies of electronic components were supplanted by the printed circuit. However, the major impetus to development came a decade later, with the introduction of the integrated circuit or 'chip'. The depositing of atoms of impurities upon wafers of silicon to reproduce the characteristics of entire circuits was to transform the computer industry. Economies of scale were generated through the possibility of mass production, which in turn led to greatly reduced unit costs per computer chip. Meanwhile, on the performance side, impressive gains in reliability and in speed of operation were to be but the forerunners of a revolution not just in the design and scale of computers but in their operation and purpose.

Hardware

Many of the most spectacular advances in computer processing occurred during the 'third generation', which lasted from the early 1960s to the early 1980s. This period witnessed the onset of large scale integration (LSI), with thousands of components fabricated on a single chip, and led to the development first of 'mini-' and then of microcomputers could outshine powerful than large mainframe computers, minicomputers could outshine them in cost-performance terms, while the appearance of the microcomputer, with one or two chips providing central processing unit (CPU), memory and input–output facilities, was to have the most far-reaching of consequences. During the third generation, moreover, distinctions between machines were reasonably clear cut with, as a rule, 'micros' having 8-bit word lengths and thus slower speeds than the 16- and 32-bits available in 'minis' and mainframe computers respectively. In the present fourth generation, when microcomputers can have word lengths of up to 32 bits, it is becoming increasingly difficult to categorise machines in the old way.[2]

Chip technology has improved so much today that developments like the transputer can serve both as computers in their own right and as programmable, plug-in components. Developed by Inmos in the United Kingdom, the transputer combines on a single chip processor, memory and communication links, as well as additional circuitry and interfaces for particular tasks, for example the control of peripherals such as printers. Its use as a programmable component could make a reality of such fifth-generation dreams as concurrency, by upgrading the processing power of existing systems by as much as a factor of ten. Moreover, using its own software language, Occam, it has tremendous networking capabilities and its ability to interconnect with other transputers could be a development of fundamental significance. The Cray-type supercomputer of today could well be replaced by a network of transputers at what would be a fraction of the cost.

Future advances in networking are likely to be aided by developments in 'wafer-scale integration' and the use of 'parallel processors'. With wafer-scale technology, circuit integration would be enhanced to the point where the existing need to interconnect chips by cutting and wiring after fabrication could be removed, with significant improvements in operating speeds. Although wafer technology is still at the development stage, parallel processing is already a fact of life. As its name implies, parallel processing involves the use of several processors at once, each performing part of a task and thus increasing speed and efficiency of operation. It seems likely that this trend will continue and that computers will have extra processors as a matter of course, assigning various tasks to free and often highly specialised processors.[2]

Memory

Computer memory embodies a number of technologies, electronic and non-electronic, the latter including a number of 'moving-surface' type memories. The major developments in electronic memory have been in storage density and access times, the former increasing dramatically to the one-megabyte-per-chip level. There have also been considerable improvements in cost, although electronic memory remains an expensive option. A further development is the availability of erasable programmable read-only memory (EPROM). This is a useful compromise between random access memory (RAM) and read only memory (ROM), providing some facility for amendment. Like ROM also it is available in plug-in form, as a kind of half-way house between hardware and software. As such it is a type of 'firmware', that is software embedded in the hardware.

The dominant form of moving-surface memory is the disk, either in hard or floppy form, providing fast, random access to large capacity storage. A second type of moving-surface memory is optical storage, whose range includes digital disks and videodisks, laser cards, bubble memories, holograms and charged couple devices, although some of these have yet to progress beyond the laboratory. Among systems in everyday use are optical digital disks and optical videodisks. In optical technology, lasers replace the read/write heads of standard moving-surface media, and the use of optical diodes helps to overcome such physical constraints as magnetic coating, head-to-surface distances and head thickness.[3]

The major drawback with this optical technology is its provision of read-only systems. However, fully erasable read and write systems to replace existing CD-ROM technology still seem to be quite a way off. While reportedly available, 'write once, read many' (WORM) systems, which enable users to write on a blank disk and replay the results, are still in short supply. Even more elusive are those 'write many, read always' (WMRA) systems, which are still largely at the development stage.[4]

Future improvements in storage technology are expected to issue from the development of dedicated processors to control storage subsystems within computer networks. It is also predicted that with the use of vertical recording of magnetic domains, storage densities will soar beyond existing maximum levels of around 11 million bits per square inch to perhaps, in say ten years' time, 400 million bits per square inch of disk storage.[5]

Input–output

The focal point of the man–machine interface, the input–output aspect of computing has changed relatively little over the years, certainly compared with other elements of computer hardware. So far as input is concerned, the major trend has been away from data entry by means of card or tape and towards the use of terminals. Other input developments include hand-held keypads, as in the Prestel system, optical character recognition, touch screens, graphics pads, mice and joysticks. There is also a range of transducers/digitisers which can transform such physical qualities as pressure or amplitude into electromagnetic impulses and then, through digitisation, into 'on-off' pulses. Output from the computer comes mainly through VDUs, or as hard copy through printers. Indeed, the continued popularity of the VDU exemplifies the relatively slow pace of change in this area of computer technology. Despite continued research into other methods of output, for the foreseeable future the VDU seems to have few realistic competitors.[3]

The pace of change has been greatest in the sphere of printing, where the virtual embarrassment of choice is perhaps best resolved on a trade-off basis between cost and performance. Daisywheel machines, which produce letter-quality print, are more expensive than thermal or dot-matrix printers, which do not. Ink-jet and laser printers are best of all for versatility, quality and speed and, not surprisingly, are high-cost options. The real breakthrough here, irrespective of the system employed, is the degree of independence from traditional commercial structures and practices which has been given to the individual. The person running a small business or the academic can now produce letter-quality copy at very competitive cost from his or her own office, without recourse to the expense and inconvenience involved in going to a third party.

Without doubt, however, the quantum leap will come with voice-activated input to, and output from, the computer. To date, progress has been more apparent in the case of voice output, which is available in both human and computerised form. Voice input is still largely a matter of isolated word recognition, where the computer can recognise a few hundred words from specified speakers. Continuous speech recognition or speech understanding systems remain very much at the research stage, essentially because of the complexities of natural language and the importance of such considerations as pitch, emphasis and context. Current techniques for digitising the human voice are not sufficiently advanced, be these waveform coders, which capture the waveform of a sound in order to reproduce it, or voice coders, which employ analysis–synthesis methods and the use of phonemes to extract those parameters of speech essential for its reproduction. If existing problems could be resolved, computers would become 'user friendly' in a way that meant something to everybody, but unfortunately this is not likely to happen overnight.

Software

In software as in hardware, there has been a tendency for old distinctions to become blurred, with, for example, systems or operating software frequently incorporating the kind of integrated facilities formerly associated with applications programs. An obvious example is the standard microcomputer package of word processing, programming, database and communications facilities. Again, while incompatibilities between systems continue, a degree of de facto standardisation now obtains in the use of operations software. However, where once CP/M (Control Program/Monitor) was the standard operating system for microcomputers, its 8-bit, single-user status has rendered it obsolete for fourth-generation use.

Recent systems have been both multiuser and multitasking, which means not only that several processors can share the same program at once, but also that the system can handle several tasks at the same time. Current operating systems include CP/M-68 and CP/M-86, which are 16-bit multitasking systems for the Motorola MC 68000 and the Intel 8086 chips respectively, and Concurrent CP/M as a 16-bit single-user operating system, adopted by IBM as PC-DOS and UNIX (and its micro derivative, XENIX).[6] Along with C, a high-level structured language, UNIX is popular with computer programmers and it incorporates special features to facilitate software development. It is a 16- or 32-bit multiuser operating system with a wide range of compiling and file-handling subsystems. Among the advantages offered by UNIX are the hierarchical structure of its file store and directories and its portability between different types of machine.[6]

At the applications level there has been a tremendous growth of software packages. This includes packages dedicated to particular functions, such as the monitoring of cardiac patients or of high-speed telecommunications networks, or general-purpose packages designed to facilitate solutions in a wide variety of areas through the provision of spreadsheet, database and graphics facilities. The pace of such development can be seen in the evolution of fourth-generation programming languages for use with 'off-the-shelf' business packages. These packages offer greater program functionality and a higher level of portability than was previously available with such high-level languages as Fortran or COBOL.[7] Through the use of such facilities as menus and windows, these fourth-generation languages are making inroads in the critical problem area of man–machine interface by helping to create a more 'user-friendly' environment. Their purpose is to make programming easier and to extend computing to the end user. Nevertheless, there remain problems of software engineering, including the construction and testing of software, proving that programs are correct, and devising and improving upon mathematical models for the 'debugging' of programs.

Despite such advances there remain serious problems arising from basic hardware incompatibilities between systems. Even though several computer systems support the same operating system, it is necessary to modify the application programs to execute under the same operating system on different types of computer.[7] Furthermore, the need to improve productivity in software and systems development is related to that for programs aimed at end users who are not computer professionals. Among the advanced development techniques currently in use are report generators and query languages, which enable end users to retrieve and manipulate data, produce reports and make use of database management systems. Even more comprehensive are applications generators, which are designed to facilitate the development of complete applications, including such facilities as database creation, file updating, report generation and query processing.[7]

It is software which, in the final analysis, holds the key to the widespread public acceptability of computers, and to success in such key areas as artificial intelligence and expert systems, for example in natural language and pattern recognition, in intelligent behaviour and user interface. As the range and sophistication of packages increase, and the trend towards the development of end-user computing continues, software is assuming a position of absolutely critical importance.

Telecommunications

As a result of the insatiable demand for high-speed communication of information and data of all kinds, the transmission of messages between remote locations has acquired a new significance in modern society. Although based upon national and international telephone networks, it is the exploitation of other, newer technologies that is creating a worldwide communications infrastructure transmitting not just voice but text, data and image as well. Although the new digital technologies render such developments at once more efficient and of higher quality than their analogue counterparts, it is rarely possible, for cost and other considerations, simply to change over from one system to the other. Therefore, when linking the two systems, for example to send digitised computer data over an analogue telephone line, it is still necessary to use a modem to make the relevant conversions from analogue to digital and vice versa. This will no longer be necessary when all telephone systems become digital.

The advent of digitisation has led to marked advances in the key areas of signal transmission and channel capacity, not least in the efficient exploitation of available bandwidth. By combining several independent data channels into a single high-speed channel, the number of communications lines required can be reduced with consequent savings in costs. This multiplexing can be effected on both a frequency and a time basis, or as some combination of both. Frequency division multiplexing involves the allocation of bandwidth among a number of narrower band uses, say by sharing a 200 MHz waveguide between speech channels, with bandwidths of 4 kHz, and television channels, which require 5.5 MHz. Time division multiplexing involves the allocation of a full bandwidth to a set of channels in turn for specified periods of time.[8]

Switching is another response to the need to share capacity among users and in so doing to reduce communication costs. In switching, where terminals are connected to the network as and when each call is made, the major advances have been in message and in packet switching. In message switching, computers monitor the network, storing messages until lines are available, then automatically re-routeing them to the required destination. The key feature is that data is broken up into pieces, that is messages, and transmitted by whichever route in the network is the most appropriate at that instant. This 'store-and-forward' system offers considerable advantages over the old circuit-switching system, not least the facility for computer monitoring and feedback for error correction and route selection. With the continued fall in computing costs, however, packet switching has emerged as the preferred mode of high-speed digital communication.[9]

In packet switching, what are transmitted are not complete messages but segments of messages, broken up into blocks or packets of data. Each packet carries the address of the message, as well as information about its own position in the message sequence. Separate packets from the same message may reach their destination by different routes. At a series of nodes along the way, receipt of the packet is acknowledged or the packet is retransmitted. At the end of the process, the packets are reassembled in their correct order by means of a device known as a pad. Packet switching exchanges (PSEs) are connected by broadband communication links and accessed by means of the switched telephone network. These PSEs carry out 'store-and-forward' and monitoring operations on the data and in general ensure that the network functions in accordance with agreed protocols for its use.[9]

Although there can still be delays between the transmission and receipt of a message, packet switching provides clear illustration of the shift from old to new technologies. Indeed, given the ability to alternate between analogue and digital transmission, and to communicate between public switched telephone networks and computer networks, this shift represents a virtual revolution in telecommunications.

Microelectronics

There is a real sense in which microelectronics comprises the core enabling technology, in that without it neither computers nor telecommunications could operate to anything like their present levels of efficiency. Indeed, many of those characteristics that are seen to typify the new technology are in fact features of microelectronics. Prominent among such features are compactness, cheapness, reliability and disposability. Of these, the most obvious feature is miniaturisation, but of even greater significance are the implications of this transformation of scale, the effects of which have filtered down to every corner of society. In essence, microelectronics has meant miniaturisation of the switch and of its related components, matters which have been touched upon earlier in this chapter. Rather than go over familiar ground again, attention will now turn away from the details of the enabling technologies to consideration of the relationship that exists between them.

Convergence

A certain amount of confusion has arisen from the fact that much of the so-called 'new technology' is not exactly novel, with, for example, telephony being over one hundred years old. However, what makes these technologies different is not just that some of them are new, but the interaction at this time between new technologies and others of older vintage. It is this process of interaction and mutual reinforcement, or in other words convergence, that is leading to truly qualitative change, to entirely new achievements and possibilities.

Convergence is a complex phenomenon, occurring simultaneously on different levels and in different directions. In its simplest form it entails straightforward technological convergence, as in the merging of telecommunications and computing in, for example, System X networks. Then there is that form of convergence which is not simply the marriage of two technologies, but leads to the erosion of functional barriers, as between, say, data processing and communications. Finally, there is the kind of convergence akin to what the economists call 'vertical integration', in which firms move backwards into industries supplying them with inputs, or forward to enter industries that purchase their outputs. This could include the entry of computer manufacturers into the online information business or, alternatively, the diversification of production into the manufacture of telephone exchanges or modems.

Irrespective of the form in which it occurs, it is convergence that both serves to explain current developments in information technology, and at the same time makes them special. Just how special can be shown by the fact that the convergence of telecommunications and computer technologies has led to the emergence of several completely new media of communication. Hence, electronic mail, online information and videotex have developed, not just as examples of communication systems, but as genres, as umbrella terms for entire new classes of interactive media. In the telecommunications field alone, the array of new technologies now includes such 'leading-edge' developments as communications satellites, fibre optics and integrated services digital networks.

Communications satellites

Satellites are communications links which are used to relay radio, television and telephone signals around the curvature of the Earth. Orbiting the Earth at a height of 35,900 kilometres and powered by solar energy, they can transmit information at speeds of millions of bits per second at costs which are virtually distance-independent. Any Earth station can communicate with any other without the need for terrestrial cabling or switching. As a result, not only telecommunications and broadcasting but international trade and market structures have undergone major transformations. In what is still a developing technology, by no means all the problems have been solved. Nevertheless, with sequentially synchronised bit streams from different Earth stations occupying the same channel, and with onboard switching between different bit streams and antennae, the power of future satellites will make that of their predecessors seem puny by comparison.[10] Such developments even hold out the promise of solutions to existing political difficulties over such matters as the allocation of slots in the geosynchronous orbit.

Fibre optics

Optic fibres could be the transmission medium of the future; hair-thin fibres of very pure glass enclosed in a plastic cable. The interface between core and cladding results in total internal reflection of light, which is then transmitted along the fibre by lasers in a series of 'on–off' pulses. The source, a transducer, converts electrical energy to light pulses and sends these along the fibre for conversion back into electronic signals by a receiving transducer. These fibres conduct light because of their transparency and owing to the fact that very little leakage occurs through the fibre wall. Their bandwidth is considerably greater than that of coaxial cable, and the non-electrical transmission mode is much less susceptible to interference.[11]

Fibre optic-based signals are transmitted in the infrared range of the spectrum, and transmission rates of up to 1,000 megabits per second have been achieved over short distances. This is currently a high-cost option, with considerable expense in the optical components and transmission devices as well as in the fibres themselves. Nevertheless, fibre optics is already making its mark in long-distance communication, where a need for fewer repeaters to boost signals gives it a decided advantage over coaxial cable. For short-range local links, on the other hand, coaxial cable will most likely continue as the economic choice for the foreseeable future.

Integrated services digital networks (ISDNs)

Networking represents one of the most tangible benefits to accrue from the converging technologies. The familiar telephone network has now developed into a resource-sharing facility linking data processing and communications resources in both local and wide area networks (LANs and WANs). These networks are distinguished by their scale, and LANs also by their considerably higher transmission speeds. The development of both types of network reflects a major expansion of data traffic and with it the integration of different information handling devices. The most spectacular manifestation of these trends has been the move towards the development of ISDNs.

Generally regarded as an evolutionary development emerging from the digitisation of public telephone facilities, ISDNs will provide a transmission service for all kinds of information formats, including voice, data, text and image. The system will work through the installation of a 'black box' or customer controller at the user's premises. This controller will be connected to a multi-bandwidth digital 'pipe' and, depending upon the application required, the controller will select the appropriate bandwidth. With its key features being intelligence and capacity, this system will present opportunities for the development of a range of completely new services and, by reducing administrative costs, it should lead to a freer flow of information.[12]

Although there are plenty of high-speed data networks in existence, for example in banking and financial services, fully integrated systems with simultaneous two-way operation are still very much at the development stage. A key problem concerns the digitisation of voice and its incorporation into data packets as part of an ISDN. Another area of difficulty is in the field of standards, where problems over different national practices, for example at the user-to-network interface, continue to retard the pace of development. There is also the problem of access to private leased lines for data transmission. Although more of a commercial than an engineering matter, it is important that such difficulties be resolved at the planning stage, otherwise potential customers could be lost, to the eventual detriment of the system.[13]

Postscript

The convergence of these enabling technologies is what makes information technology such an important force in society. It really does seem to be one of those cases where the whole turns out to be greater than the sum of the parts. There is an important corollary, however, which is that the truly revolutionary impact of these technologies is to be found in their social and economic manifestations. The wider policy implications of technological convergence are dealt with in Chapter 9, so at this point it remains only to emphasise its critical contribution to the development of modern economies.

In the United Kingdom, the official response has been twofold: liberalisation of telecommunications, as the essential infrastructure of economic growth; and creation of a policy for advanced information technology. So far as telecommunications are concerned, this has led to the 'privatisation' of the industry, the introduction of a limited amount of competition through the licensing of Mercury Communications and Hull Telephones, and establishment of the Office of Telecommunications (OfTel) as a 'watchdog' body. As regards the wider field of information technology, the main Government response has been creation of the Alvey Directorate, with funding of £350 million to enhance United Kingdom capabilities in the key areas of software engineering, man–machine interface, very large scale integration and intelligent knowledge-based systems. This programme has enjoyed a reasonable amount of success, especially in fostering collaborative research and development work involving industry and the academic community. However, the level of funding has always been distinctly modest in relation to the stated aims of the programme, and as it nears the end of its first five years of existence, the Government seems to be demurring over the nature of any future initiative. Whatever happens, however, there seems little likelihood of any falling off in either the influence or the importance of information technology.

References

1. Great Britain, Department of Trade and Industry, *Information technology: the age of electronic information*, London, HMSO, 1982, 1.
2. Lucas, Henry C., *Introduction to computers and information systems*, New York, Macmillan, 1985, 122.
3. Cawkell, A. E., Information technology and communications, in *Annual review of information science & technology*, vol. 15, ed. M. E. Williams, White Plains, New York, Knowledge Industry Publications, 1979, 37–65.
4. Falk, Howard, Hardware corner: optical disk storage, *The Electronic Library*, 4, 1, 1986, 20–23.
5. Lucas, op. cit., 523.
6. Clifton, H. D., *Business data systems*, 3rd ed., Englewood Cliffs, New Jersey, Prentice Hall, 1986, 167.
7. Lucas, op. cit., 179–83.
8. Reynolds, George W., *Introduction to business telecommunications*, Columbus, Ohio, Merril, 1984, 14–23.
9. Zorkoczy, Peter, *Information technology: an introduction*, New York, Van Nostrand, 1984, 51–61.
10. Cawkell, op. cit., 1980, 39.
11. *Concise Oxford science dictionary*, London, OUP, 1984, 681.
12. Harris, L. and E. Davis, System X and the evolving U.K. telecommunications network, *The Post Office Engineers Journal*, 72, 2, April 1979, 7–13.
13. Burgess, B. C., 'ISDN and the digital future: user requirements in the marketplace'. Paper presented at the Annual Conference of the Pacific Telecommunications Council, Honolulu, 15 January 1985. Unpublished.

CHAPTER 4

The information society

We live in an age of information, a time when the destinies of people and nations are dependent as never before on a factor as elusive in concept as it is intangible in substance. And yet, information is all around us, in the air, under the oceans and in outer space. This is the message not just of the media or of professional futurologists but also of industry, the trade unions and government. Information is the basis of economic growth, and the essential characteristic and driving force of a range of technologies of breathtaking potential. It is hardly surprising, therefore, that the link with information should now have been extended to embrace society itself. This chapter explores the basic idea of society as information society. It examines the evolution and present status of the concept and assesses its general validity as a way of looking at society.

An initial categorisation

It has been customary to categorise society in some sort of fashion over the years, with designations such as 'open' or 'closed', 'agrarian' or 'industrial' serving as useful indicators of the kind of society in question. Although there has been no sustained attempt so far by sociologists to construct a theory of the information society, the term itself is widely used, albeit in a general and unscientific manner. In a casual, everyday context it is just as valid to talk about 'information societies' as about any other type of society. Used thus, the term is a kind of shorthand, denoting societies at an advanced stage of development. Where something more specific is intended, however, it is important to ensure that the terminology employed relates precisely to the circumstances it purports to describe. Thus, if what is meant is an entire transformation of society and its recasting in an information context, then clearly a fair degree of specificity in definition and, indeed, caution in use, will be required.

This chapter is concerned more with the latter approach to the concept, and with the contention that changes of a fundamental nature are taking place within society. As a precursor to consideration of these changes, therefore, let us start with an initial categorisation of the information society. As generally understood, the information society is an advanced, postindustrial society of a type found most commonly in the West. It is characterised by a high degree of computerisation and large volumes of electronic data transmission, and by an economic profile heavily influenced by the market and employment possibilities of information technology.

Why 'information society'?

The ways in which the concept of the information society have been expressed have attracted a fair amount of criticism, usually on the grounds of ambiguity or unsuitability. Hence, Kochen writes of criticism over an alleged loss of meaning through overuse of the term, which, he observes, is in any event only one of several possible scenarios for the future.[1] However, neither the 'information society' nor its equivalent terms are to be taken too literally, but should rather be employed as indicators of the nature and direction of changes in society. Dizard has provided a useful listing of such terms, and for present purposes his 'information age' will be seen as coterminous with Bell's 'postindustrial society' and the concept favoured here, the 'information society'.[2]

Such criticism can be expected to continue, however, and not just in terms of future developments, but as regards the labels we attach to social change. Arguably, where people think about these matters at all it is more likely to be in terms of democratic or totalitarian societies, socialist or capitalist societies, or societies characterised by affluence, poverty or unemployment, rather than by information. In any case, it could be asked, why now? Information in some form has existed and been highly valued in every age. It was essential to the march of progress in preindustrial times and during the Industrial Revolution, and so it remains today. So why 'information society'?

In some respects this might seem to be a pointless question, bearing in mind the vast quantities of information, the sheer amount of research and development activity, that underpins all those advances in computers and telecommunications that so many now take for granted. Communications satellites, the electronic office, the home delivery of computer-based information and entertainment services – surely here is proof enough to render the question redundant? Well at one level perhaps, but then why not a 'scientific' or a 'high-tech' society? In any event, is this not a somewhat narrow basis for the kind of generalised social change that is implicit in use of the term 'information society'?

Perusal of the literature of the information society would tend to support this suspicion of narrowness, and would indicate a certain vulnerability to charges of materialism and technological determinism. This difficulty arises from the nature of the new information technology and its role in an information society. Hence, while we have been anticipating the coming of the information society for over 20 years, a preoccupation with technology and its applications may have left us unprepared for the consideration of wider social issues.[3] This may be partly explained by the eagerness of governments to exploit the potential of the new technology, with a concern for short-term political advantage obscuring the true significance of the change that is taking place.[4] That this change is based on an intrinsically revolutionary technology, differing not merely in degree but in kind from other such developments in our time, is an indication both of its magnitude and of the apparent failure of many, governments included, to fully comprehend its meaning.[5]

This is not so much a failure to understand as it is a failure of communications, a particular irony in the context of a new kind of society emergent on a revolutionary mix of electronics and telecommunications technologies. The fact remains that the message of the information society, as society, still has considerable ground to make up on the progress made in its techno-economic manifestations. Any balanced assessment of societal status would of necessity have to account not only for the way in which societies earn their living but also for general attitudes towards right and wrong, and for concepts of community, social status, property and institutions.

Studying the information society

Any attempt at studying the information society must at some point address two quite fundamental issues: whether the context is that of the present or the future, and the need for some measure of consensus on the matter of terminology. On the first point, such is the extent to which the term has entered everyday use that one could be forgiven for thinking that the information society was already a fact of life, at least in the developed nations.* Indeed, the best-selling American author Naisbett is sufficiently confident of his ground as to state that the transformation from industrial to information society began in the 1960s.[6] Naisbett was primarily concerned with events in the United States and it would be unwise to generalise from this particular case, however important it might be. On the other hand, there is no lack of supporting evidence elsewhere, notably in the case of Japan, which is arguably the archetypal information society.

Even in Japan, however, there is more than a touch of futurism to this issue, with scholars like Masuda anticipating an essentially social transformation to the point where so-called 'information values' provide the formative force for

---

* During 1983, both *New Society* and *Political Quarterly* gave the subject sufficient attention to support this contention. In both instances, the term 'information society' was used as a matter of course.

the development of society.[7] These goals entail the full realisation of individual human potential, something later reiterated by Kochen, who emphasised the importance of information in reflecting such societal invariants as the value of individual freedom for United States society.[8] That this is not entirely a matter of science fiction is evident in those changes that are taking place in the social, as well as in the physical, infrastructure of a number of countries. Nevertheless, there is still some way to go before Masuda's 'Computopia' materialises or, indeed, a very different alternative, an 'automated state' in which everything is controlled by computers.[9] Whatever the outcome, however, the context is clearly that of the future.

What then of the matter of terminology and, specifically, of that need for consensus that was identified as the second fundamental issue attending the study of the information society? Any such consensus, if it is to come, will be founded on two broad groups of opinion: those people who accept the concept of an information society, and those who, while not totally convinced, are at least prepared to maintain an open mind on the subject. Others will continue to be sceptical, regarding the concept as meaningless or at best unhelpful, and if they do not subscribe to the notion in the first place, there would seem little point in seeking their cooperation in the matter of terminology.

No matter how one regards the concept, it still requires something of an act of faith to advance the notion of a society in which information is the truly independent variable. To do so is to raise issues of virtually an ideological nature and, in effect, to reduce dramatically the list of potential candidates for information society status. It would also do much to resolve any remaining doubts about the timescale involved, about whether the information society exists in the present or lies in the future. If, on the other hand, what is envisaged is a society in which information is emerging as a new or newly appreciated variable, capable of affecting other variables and enhancing the overall quality of life, then one is faced with a much more realistic proposition.

Irrespective of the scenario which is being painted, it would greatly assist in the general understanding of the information society if it could be assessed in a 'real world' context. Dordick has made a useful contribution to this process of understanding. He suggests that, rather than viewing the process in absolute terms, we should envisage societies as featuring on a continuum leading by stages towards the information society.[10] Progress along this continuum can then be assessed in terms of such variables as level of information consciousness, the environment for information processing, the development of information sectors or economies, and the emergence of information-related goals and values. To overlook these gradations in development is to overtax such consensus on terminology as exists, and makes the study of the information society an even more difficult task.

Criteria for the information society

In view of the amount of attention paid to the subject in recent years, the nature and, to some extent, the dimensions of the information society ought to be well-enough known. However, if comparisons are to be made, and countries are to be assessed for information society status, then some knowledge of the conditions or criteria required becomes necessary. Although such criteria exist, they tend to be implicit and unstated rather than enumerated in formal or deliberate fashion. Nonetheless, the Nora–Minc report in France clearly envisaged a link between technological and social concerns, between converging telecommunications and data processing technologies and policies for social and economic development.[11] In outlining his 'Computopia', Masuda laid down a framework for society based upon innovative technology, socioeconomic structure and values,[12] while the European Community's Forecasting and Assessment in Science and Technology (FAST) programme on the information society recognises the interplay between techno-industrial and social issues.[13]

Table 1. Criteria for the development of an information society	
Technological criteria	IT as the key enabling force. Widespread diffusion of IT in offices, factories, education and the home.
Social criteria	Information as an enhancer of the quality of life. Widespread information consciousness and end-user access to high-quality information.
Economic criteria	Information as key economic factor: as resource, service, commodity, a source of added value and employment.
Political criteria	Freedom of information leading to a political process characterised by increased participation and consensus.
Cultural criteria	Recognition of the cultural value of information through the promotion of information values in the interests of national and individual development.

Dubbing this interplay the 'dual challenge', and anxious that technology be contained within a broader social and cultural context, rather than the other way round, this European initiative not only lays down criteria but also asserts the importance of cultural and social parameters within them. The FAST programme has identified five strategic issues for the information society: key technologies, Europe's position in the international information and communication system, alienation or integration in an information society, employment, and education and training.[13]

It is against this background that the criteria for the development of an information society, presented in Table 1, were assembled. In this list, few individual criteria would be mutually exclusive, with each referring to a subclass rather than to one discrete or finite criterion.

This list of potential criteria is offered more by way of illustration than anything else, and certainly makes no claims to completeness. While decidedly future-orientated, it contains sufficient recognisable elements to permit general state-of-the-art assessments of progress towards the development of an information society. Such assessments would benefit from an additional set of inputs, which would be quantitative indicators drawn from the list as a whole, including numbers of computers of all kinds, estimates of the scale of transborder dataflow, statistics on the information industry, the share of information activities in the gross national product (GNP) and in the workforce, penetration by media of all kinds, and numbers of people engaged in education and training.

What is the information society?

There is now a sufficient volume of writing on the topic to support attempts at finding a consensus on the nature and characteristics of the information society. In a sense, the worldwide currency of the concept represents de facto recognition, which in itself is a form of consensus. Again, with due regard for differences in national approaches, there has been considerable uniformity of response to the challenge of the information society in such international fora as the Organisation for Economic Cooperation and Development (OECD) and the European Economic Community (EEC).

Within the framework of the OECD, a distinction can be drawn between the approach taken by the Japanese on the one hand, and by the Americans and Western Europeans on the other. It would be wrong to overstate this distinction, which on occasion is more a matter of degree than of kind, but it does exist. Thus, while all concerned are committed to the achievement of an advanced society with a sophisticated telecommunications infrastructure and a wealth-creating information technology sector, the Japanese display a particular awareness of the social and cultural implications of information development. This is nowhere more apparent than in the writings of Masuda, which, at times almost mystical in tone, are a constant reminder of the enormous qualitative changes inherent in moving from an industrial to an information society. Hence, while the Nora–Minc report in France was quite rightly hailed as a breakthrough in understanding the full social and political ramifications of the new technologies, it came more than a decade after the Japanese produced their plan for a future information society.[14] The breadth of vision inherent in such activities must surely help to explain Japanese success in those more material aspects of the information society targeted for action by other nations.

In attempting to reach some generally acceptable definition of the information society, therefore, certain points should be borne in mind. First is the value of the continuum approach outlined above, with societies progressing towards more advanced stages of development, including that of the information society, at their own pace and with varying results. Second is the need to include consideration of wider social and even philosophical issues in arriving at a definition, such issues as the quality of life in a highly technocratic society. Third is the temporal context, and the fact that one is almost certainly talking about future rather than current developments.

Having said all this, however, the value of current developments should not be overlooked, and already there are sufficient indications of information-driven social change to lend some form of credibility to notions of an information society. These would include: structural economic change, particularly as regards distribution of the labour force; an increased awareness of the value of the information resource; a growing appreciation of the need for widespread computer literacy; the wholesale diffusion of information technologies; and government intervention in support of the key enabling technologies of computing, microelectronics and telecommunications.

Therefore, in the context of existing developments in the advanced industrial nations, one would define the information society as one in which the quality of life, as well as prospects for social change and economic development, depend increasingly on information and its exploitation. In such a society, living standards, patterns of work and leisure, the education system and the marketplace are all influenced markedly by advances in information and knowledge. This is evidenced by an increasing array of information-intensive products and services, communicated through a wide range of media, many of them electronic in nature.

Prospects for an information society

In attempting to clarify the nature and development of information societies, this chapter has been set in the context of advanced Western nations, possessed of the necessary technological, sociopolitical and human resources. Time and progress should widen this perspective to include countries in the Eastern bloc and within the developing world. For the time being, the general criteria for the development of information societies are clearly beginning to emerge, especially in countries such as Japan and the United States. Japan has probably made most progress in this regard, aided by its essential cultural cohesiveness and by a determination to succeed that is shared by industry, government, the academic and research communities, and apparently by the public at large. Developments in the United States may have been less coherent but, nevertheless, they have set the pace for technological and social change all over the world.

The momentum gained by the Japanese and the American challenge has evoked a series of responses from European nations, acting both on their own and in concert through the EEC.* The extent to which such efforts succeed should go some considerable way to determining not only the survival of the European information industry but also the attainment and future shape of the information and communications technologies and services;[15] an interactive infrastructure of technology, markets and politics;[16] a society where technology transfer, questions of transborder dataflow and of the political and cultural sovereignty of nations, are dealt with in the concluding chapters of this book. The present chapter ends where it began, with a final look at the central theme of the volume – the concept of an information society.

A viable concept?

For good or ill, the concept of an information society has now gained a fair degree of acceptance; a currency which, at least in part, is related to the everyday utility of the term. That this measure of support for the concept stops some way short of definitional consensus need not be a deterrent to the use of the term. If anything, in fact, the more varied the approach, the better is likely to be the overall level of understanding. 'Telematique', or the combination of information and communications technologies and services;[15] an interactive infrastructure of technology, markets and politics;[16] a society where information is central to social development and organisational management;[17] or one where access to information, for everybody, is guaranteed[18] – these are all valid and mutually sustaining perceptions, which, irrespective of their place on the conceptual and developmental spectra, provide a useful instrument for social observation. This instrument, the concept of an information society, still has some way to go before it becomes a

---

* Examples already mentioned are the Alvey Programme (UK), Nora–Minc (France), and FAST (EEC); another EEC initiative, ESPRIT, is discussed in Chapter 9.

reality rather than a plausible social construct. As a concept, however, it is certainly viable.

References

1. Kochen, Manfred, Information and society, in *Annual review of information science & technology*, vol. 18, ed. M. E. Williams, White Plains, New York, 1983, 277–304.

2. Dizard, Wilson P., The coming information age, *The Information Society Journal*, 1, 2, 1981, 91–112.

3. Mitchell, Jeremy, The information society: private monopolies and the public interest, *Political Quarterly*, 54, 1983, 160–67.

4. Tracy, Michael, Telecommunications: effects on existing media, *Political Quarterly*, 54, 1983, 177–86.

5. Gosling, William, Information technology's seven league boots, *Political Quarterly*, 54, 1983, 120–26.

6. Naisbett, John, *Megatrends: ten new directions transforming our lives*, New York, Warner Books, 1984, 1.

7. Masuda, Yoneji, Computopia, in *The information technology revolution*, ed. Tom Forester, Oxford, Blackwell, 1985, 620–34.

8. Kochen, op. cit., 280.

9. Masuda, op. cit., 620.

10. Dordick, Herbert, Information society indicators: description, measurement, prediction, in *Information societies: comparing the Japanese and the American experiences*, ed. A.S. Adelstein et al., Seattle, International Communications Centre, 1978, 279.

11. Nora, Simon and Alain Minc, *The computerisation of society: a report to the President of France*, Cambridge, Massachusetts, MIT Press, 1980.

12. Masuda, op. cit., 622.

13. Grewlich, Klaus and Finn Pedersen, eds., *Power and participation in an information society*, Luxembourg, Commission of the European Communities, 1984, 9.

14. Tateno, Tadao, Telecommunications administration in Japan, in Adelstein et al., op. cit., 9.

15. Sweeney, Gerry P., Telematics and development, *The Information Society Journal*, 1, 2, 1981, 113–30.

16. Cawkell, Anthony E., ed., *Handbook of information technology and office systems*, Amsterdam, North Holland, 1986, 369.

17. Cronin, Blaise, Personal communication, March, 1986.

18. Garfield, Eugene, Everyday problems in an information society, in Cawkell, op. cit., *Handbook*, 883–88.

CHAPTER 5

The social impact of information technology

In this chapter, attention will focus upon the social impact of information technology within developed Western societies. Those aspects of social impact of particular concern to developing nations are given separate treatment in Chapter 9. In both cases, social impact will be taken as referring to the influence of the new information technology upon the overall development of society and on the quality of life of its citizens. The impacts occur at both the individual and the organisational level, in a wide range of social situations, at work and in the home. This interaction between technology and society is frequently subject to a range of legislative or regulatory controls, measures which in themselves are an indicator of social impact.

Not that the effect of the technologies is always so apparent. Hence, where the development of home computing is clearly a matter of some social significance, less obvious is the diffusion of ubiquitous chip technology by means of a wide range of more mundane domestic appliances, such as toasters, washing machines and microwave ovens. The fact that this is in many cases concealed technology, with the users largely unaware of its existence, in no way diminishes its importance in terms of social impact. More obvious is the psychological impact of information technology, with reaction ranging from wholehearted support for technological innovation to outright rejection, on the basis of its perceived threat to work and employment. For good or ill, however, there can be no gainsaying the social impact of information technology. It is a force which is not just transforming the lives of entire communities but also helping to redefine the entire context of relations between nations.

Cronin has provided a comprehensive description of the social impact of information technology, using concepts such as 'mystification' and 'transformation'.[1] In order to understand the full implications of such concepts, however, it is necessary to turn to the issues contained within them, issues whose outcome will determine the shape and tenor of the information society. It should be emphasised that, in this case, use of the term 'issues' does not necessarily imply that these are 'problem issues'. Although much of the debate on social impact does in fact focus upon technology-related problems, it is worth remembering that there have been widespread benefits attending the introduction of information technology. Whether positive or negative in connotation, and with due allowance for overlap and the converging nature of the information technologies, these issues can be categorised as either regulatory, commercial or human in character.

Regulatory issues

While possessing obvious political and commercial characteristics, the social ramifications of regulation extend into such fundamental areas as access to information and freedom of choice. The most prominent sphere of regulatory activity is probably that of telecommunications, with the deregulation of the American Telephone and Telegraph Company (AT&T) attracting attention all over the world. As from January 1984, AT&T lost some two-thirds of its assets through the divesting of its 22 local telephone companies and their reorganisation into seven separate companies, each serving a specific region of the United States.

This was an historic decision against a company which is a household name in the United States, and whose origins go back to the founding of the Bell Telephone Company in 1877. It is now the largest corporation in the world, with interests in telecommunications, manufacturing, information services and research. In a previous anti-trust suit, launched by the United States Justice Department in 1949 but unresolved until 1956, AT&T and its operating subsidiaries were prohibited from engaging in business other than communications common carrier services, that is telecommunications services to the general public. The action which led to deregulation in 1984, a further anti-trust suit, initiated by the Justice Department a decade before, succeeded in breaking-up the system by divestiture of its 22 Bell Operating Companies (BOCs).[2] Although this removed AT&T's near-monopoly position in local telephone service, the company remains the dominant provider of long-distance services and, more significantly, it has been permitted entry into previously prohibited markets in such fields as data processing, computer communications and equipment sales.

Whereas, throughout its existence, AT&T had been a target for anti-trust actions, from private as well as government sources, by the mid-1980s a significant new factor had come into play. This was the sheer enabling potential of the new technology, which in effect made nonsense of monopolistic or heavily regulated trading arrangements. In the United States, regulation of communications began in the early years of this century, with the purpose of ensuring an efficient common carrier service, operating to agreed technical and business standards in the wider public interest. Arrangements which were perfectly satisfactory when telecommunications was a single-product industry, using a relatively stable technology, simply became overtaken by social and technological change.[2] Hence, by the 1980s, it no longer made sense to provide telecommunications services on the basis of heavily regulated public utilities, and there was an irresistible build up of pressure for deregulation and the anticipated benefits of increased competition.

This point about competition is important because, in the United States as elsewhere, telecommunications had long been regarded as a natural monopoly. Natural monopolies occur where the supply conditions permit single-operator provision on the basis of certain economies of scale, which can then be passed on to the consumer. The behaviour of this monopoly provider is then controlled in the public interest, either through regulation, as in the United States, or, as has happened in Europe, through nationalisation of the company.[2] In the United States, where deregulation had been gathering momentum since the 1950s, the trend has been towards the break-up of those markets in which natural monopoly conditions no longer apply. Examples include the telephone equipment market and the advanced services sector, where computer processing is applied to the format, content, code or protocol of the information transmitted for subscribers.[2] This deregulation of the common carrier networks is intended to help the business user by creating the conditions for a lowering of charges, an improvement in service, and a higher rate of technological innovation.

In the United Kingdom, where the process is known as 'liberalisation', similar forces have been at work. Here, too, the primary focus of attention has been on the telecommunications system where until 1981 British Telecom had a complete monopoly on all stages in the telecommunications process, either directly or through licensing. Following publication of the Beesley report on the liberalisation of telecommunications, the Post Office and British Telecom were given separate identities, and a year later, in 1982, a second network provider, Mercury Communications, was licensed. It was also decided to 'privatise' British Telecom and it was floated on the Stock Market in 1985.[2] Such developments notwithstanding, it was realised that British Telecom would continue to dominate the market in the United Kingdom for many years to come and that, accordingly, there would still be a need for some kind of regulation. This resulted in the convening of the Littlechild Committee on the regulation of profitability in British Telecom, and led to the creation, in 1985, of the Office of the Director-General for Telecommunications (OfTel).

The framework for liberalisation in the United Kingdom was provided by the Telecommunications Acts of 1981 and 1984. The 1981 Act effected the separation of the telecommunications and the postal services. The 1984 Act paved the way for privatisation and for a form of regulatory structure that would protect the consumer from the worst excesses of market competition. In the light of such events, it might be inferred that the deregulation process has succeeded, and that a telecommunications environment adequate for the 1980s has been the result. However, things are not always what they seem and, arguably, what has happened has been as much a matter of re-regulation as anything else. Thus, in the case of the United Kingdom, the appearance of a second network provider, Mercury Communications, coupled with the prohibition of further entry to this market before 1990, seems hardly calculated to institute cut-throat competition. Indeed, it is possible that in a market occupied by only one or two firms, those involved might seek to have a form of re-regulation enacted, both to protect their profits and to make further entry to the market a difficult process.[3] In the United States, meanwhile, far from curbing the power of AT&T, the opening up of local telecommunications markets has seen the company diversify into the unregulated market for business systems and equipment.

Furthermore, in neither the United Kingdom nor the United States has deregulation been a uniform affair. There has been a tendency to differentiate between data processing, which has been unregulated, and communications services, which have been heavily regulated. This was a major conclusion of the US Federal Communications Commission's (FCC) first Computer Enquiry. However, Computer Enquiry 2 drew a further distinction, between basic communications services and enhanced communications services. In this case, basic services would continue to be subject to regulation, while enhanced services, apart from those provided by AT&T, would not.[2] In the event, AT&T was still able to enter the unregulated areas of computing and data processing, simply by meeting a requirement that it set up a separate company for the purpose.

Therefore, while the deregulation of telecommunications has introduced a modicum of competition to the market, and helped to widen the range of products and services available, it has been a far from unqualified success. In the United Kingdom, OfTel has been criticised for its weakness and lack of effectiveness in its oversight of the new competitive arrangements,[4] while disputes between providers and users of services are commonplace the world over. In such cases, the providers are the established common carriers, and the users are either companies dependent upon telecommunications services or equipment, or firms which are themselves seeking to become common carriers. As a rule, these disputes are over issues of interconnection, standardisation and cross-subsidisation.

Interconnection

Interconnection involves the rights of customers to connect their own equipment to the network, irrespective of its make or type. It was not until the FCC ruled in 1968, against the refusal by AT&T to allow the Carter Electronic Corporation to connect its mobile radio system to the telephone network, that the first major breakthrough was made in this very important field. This so-called 'Carterphone ruling' was a critical decision in terms of its implications for freedom of choice and public access to the telephone system. Although it by no means solved all the problems, it resulted in clear and demonstrable benefits to users through opening the way for deployment of all manner of equipment, including private telephone exchanges, mobile exchanges, terminals, modems and telephone handsets. In the United Kingdom, the British Approvals Board for Telecommunications (BABT) was established under the terms of the 1981 Telecommunications Act with the job of approving all apparatus for connection to the network. Only apparatus bearing its approved mark may be connected. Unapproved apparatus may be marketed, but it must bear an official prohibition mark and, consequently, it is illegal to attach such apparatus to the network.

Standardisation

The continuing debate over standards is one of the clearest indications that serious problems remain to be solved. In this case, standardisation refers to the need for agreement on the use and interconnection of different kinds of equipment, both within individual countries and on an international basis. This is an area rife in commercial and political pressures, particularly at the international level, where, for example, different countries have applied their own standards to the testing of equipment. In the search for some form of agreement it is important that a balance be maintained between flexibility and control, ensuring that standardisation does not occur at the expense of effort or initiative. There are two aspects to the problem: the actual setting of standards, and homologation or the business of applying them.

One result of technological convergence has been a pressing need for agreement on the matter of design and interface standards for data communication networks. This includes standards for hardware and software, as well as for system architecture, performance and protocols.[5] In the crucial area of protocols (rules and conventions for data transmission between two communications networks) considerable hopes are resting on the success of open systems interconnection (OSI). This set of protocols has seven layers or functions, ranging from the bottom layer, the 'plug and socket' level, to the top layer, which represents the fine detail of applications, such as the number of characters displayed on a line.[6] This seven-layered set of protocols has been agreed by the International Standards Organisation (ISO), the International Telephone and Telegraph Consultative Committee (CCITT), and the Institute of Electrical and Electronics Engineering (IEEE). Its prospects for acceptance have been enhanced by a requirement that all equipment included in contracts for both the United States and the United Kingdom governments must be up to OSI standard.

Related developments in interface protocols include IBM's system network architecture (SNA) and the CCITT's X-25 protocol. The former, which uses packet switching and embodies an equivalent of virtually all the OSI layers with the possible exception of the last one, is expensive and ties the user to IBM equipment or to expensively modified compatibles. The X-25 protocol will eventually provide for packet-switched communication compatible with the bottom four layers of OSI, on public and private networks.[6] Along with similar advances, such as the CCITT's X-400 protocol for messaging and document delivery, and OSI, these rules for interconnection will eventually culminate in protocols for ISDNs.

In fact, ISDNs provide a useful illustration of the difficulties inherent in the search for standardisation. Telecommunications administrations, equipment manufacturers and user organisations are all trying to come to grips with a range of practical difficulties in this area, including those of network functions, interfaces and performance levels. The principal objective of such deliberations ought to be the promotion of a relatively limited set of worldwide standards, defining access to ISDNs as well as their functional performance characteristics. As things stand, the overall aim of single-network accessibility is being frustrated by a proliferation of product and system incompatibilities. At the international level, there are substantial differences between Europe and the United States in their approach to standardisation. Indeed, even within Europe, in 1984, the CCITT adopted over 30 recommendations in the area of customer interface alone. Although certain interim decisions were subsequently reached, the next major batch of standards for interface and network functions is not expected until 1988.

Cross-subsidisation

In the matter of cross-subsidisation, also, the difficulties are persistent and by no means easily resolved. Cross-subsidisation entails the use of revenues earned in one enterprise to subsidise the activities of another. It is a continuing source of conflict in an industry with a high social and political profile. Cross-subsidies can come in a variety of forms and, depending upon who or what is being subsidised and how, they can be seen as being either for or against the wider public interest. In the United Kingdom, it is the principle of cross-subsidisation that supports the provision of otherwise nonviable telecommunications services, for example the maintenance of telephone kiosks in remote rural areas. In the United States, on the other hand, there has been criticism of certain telephone companies who have allegedly used the revenues derived from local monopolies to subsidise operations in more competitive markets.

As a final word on these regulatory issues, it should perhaps be observed that they have still to run their course. In the United Kingdom, the liberalisation of telecommunications has turned out to be a disappointment, in terms of both user charges and general service development. In the United States, the deregulation process is, in fact, regarded as being at an early stage, with the need for a transitional period for the movement from regulated telecommunications monopolies to deregulated competition to take place.[7] The need is all the more apparent in view of the fact that the environment concerned has now far outgrown the domain of telecommunications. However, such matters can ultimately be resolved only at the policy-making level and, in fact, telecommunications and data processing are increasingly emerging as features of national information policies.

Commercial issues

Inevitably, in view of the overlapping nature of these three categories, consideration of the commercial aspects of the social impact will touch upon matters already raised elsewhere. These commercial aspects comprise that complex of market and other relationships consequent upon developments in the information and communications technologies and the emergence of an information industry. As most of these developments are explored in later chapters, the immediate focus of interest will be at the broader analytical level.

In the first place, it would be difficult to exaggerate the commercial significance of these converging technologies. Telecommunications is now widely acknowledged not just as an important sector in its own right but also as the central nervous system of the international economy. Key industries, such as manufacturing, banking and insurance, airlines and computer services, are dependent on the rapid and efficient flow of data communications. It can be argued that these are merely service industries, and that, in any case, there is an essential qualitative difference between data and information. Apart from one's personal dislike of such distinctions, which are examined in detail in Chapter 1, and the fact that the technology employed is itself acknowledged to be informational in character, these criticisms would seem to overlook one essential point: the nature and intention of these transactions are informational, be they in the form of market futures, credit transfers or airline reservations.

In the second place, telecommunications, computers and microelectronics are combining to provide a world market in information goods and services: in computer hardware and software, in switching and transmission equipment and, not least, in professional knowledge and expertise. Not surprisingly, this global marketplace is prey to all manner of imperfections, including hidden subsidies and monopolies, international cartels, and a wide range of legal, technical and political barriers to trade. Moreover, as the stakes are high, the risks for those losing out in the competition for markets are more than commensurate. The deregulation of telecommunications may, indeed, lead to increased competition in the public interest, but will the wider national interest be served if this results in an influx of imported goods and services? The implications of such developments for trade and employment are not lost on national governments.

A further social implication of the emergence of these international markets is the growing tendency towards treating information as a commodity. This extends not just to the marketing of new forms of information but also to the 'privatisation' of material previously available without charge from public sources. This is an issue which embraces both philosophical and commercial perspectives and which, as a result, has proved to be highly contentious. Many would see an inherent injustice in a situation which entails bringing information into the marketplace, thereby in effect replacing the need to know with the ability to pay. In such circumstances, the exercise of consumer sovereignty could mean that those who were able to pay for information would eventually become the arbiters of what is to be provided, on what terms and to whom. On the other hand, as information is clearly a resource which can be used to generate additional resources, there are many who would argue for its exploitation on a commercial basis, with the provision of the necessary safeguards in terms of public access.

Finally in this section on commercial issues, there is the impact of information technology on users. In the computing field, this can be summarised in terms of an increasing flexibility and versatility in systems, with desktop technology and evermore 'intelligent' software bringing about the rise of the 'end user'. In telecommunications, the major impacts have also been felt in the interface between users and the system. Traditionally, the emphasis here has been upon questions of supply and of access to markets for equipment and services. As a result, discussions have been dominated over the years by the service providers and equipment manufacturers, with little input from the business user, let alone from the domestic customer.

Objections to this state of affairs have arisen not just on grounds of equity but for more practical reasons as well. The principal argument for user participation in high-level technological discussions has been that stressing the importance of feedback between users and providers. It is the users who suffer most from problems of system incompatibility or from restrictions on operation and access. At a wider level, moreover, it is users who bear the brunt of modifications to the general social role of national telecommunications administrations, or PTTs. This could happen if, for example, large private networks were permitted to compete with national undertakings, thus eroding PTT profits and eventually necessitating some reduction in service levels.

Human issues

A recurring theme in the literature of the information society is a comparison with the circumstances obtaining during the Industrial Revolution. Most commonly, reference is made to some new incarnation of those earlier times, say the 'New Industrial Revolution' or the 'Second Industrial Revolution'. Whatever the verdict on such comparisons, there is an unmistakable similarity in the tenor of the observations. Particularly noticeable is a clear division of opinion between what might be termed 'optimists' and 'pessimists' – between those who are broadly in favour of the development of an information society and those who would prefer for it not to happen.

In publicising their case, the optimists appear to have been the more effective, with writers such as Bell, Naisbett, Toffler and Masuda attaining best-seller status. In Masuda's view, society will undergo dramatic changes typified not by struggles, wars and revolutions but by systematic, orderly transformation.[8] Less familiar, but equally valid, are the views of the pessimists, people who, like earlier critics of the Industrial Revolution, tend to come from the Left of the political spectrum. Thus, says Robbins, information technology should be seen not in terms of futuristic utopias and technological revolutions, but as a further stage in the subordination of social needs and values to technological rationalisation and the needs of the market.[9] Echoing these sentiments, Garnham contrasted two forms of society: one based on social reciprocity and what he termed the public essence of humanity; the other on the private world of commodity-based exchange and capitalist domination.[10]

Politics aside, it is interesting to note the amount of common ground that obtains in respect of these information-related issues. Distrust of the activities of multinational corporations such as IBM, AT&T and Xerox is widespread, as is the belief that most of the social costs of the information society will be borne by the workforce.[11] Nevertheless, there is always the danger alluded to earlier that the more dramatic, and frequently the negative, aspects of change will be overemphasised at the expense of a more balanced interpretation of events. Rapid socioeconomic change of the type precipitated by advances in information technology can involve the population in new roles which conflict with traditional values and which, while subtle in their impact, are as yet dimly understood.[12]

Specific social and legal issues

Attention now turns to some of the more specific impacts, and in particular to certain problem areas arising from the onset of information technology. These problems stem either from use of the technology or from conflicting perceptions of the issues which it raises. Some of these issues, such as transborder dataflow, are dealt with in later chapters. Those considered here are privacy, freedom of information, computer crime, intellectual property, vulnerability, and alienation.

Privacy

The principle of personal privacy is one of the basic hallmarks of a democratic society. Over the years, however, the concept has been amended. Where once it meant the freedom of each individual to be left alone, it now extends to cover possible infringements of this privacy arising from the application of information technology. This interference can come from government and other institutional sources as well as from individuals.

There are two essential aspects to this issue of personal privacy. The first is the protection of individual citizens from intrusions into their private lives. The second concerns potential intrusion through the misuse of personal information disclosed voluntarily by the injured party. In modern societies, citizens are required to make all manner of personal information available to any number of sources. Whether this be in respect of employment, credit status or state benefits, or in fulfilment of electoral or census obligations, the information-gathering process is one which is very open to abuse. The relative ease with which such data can be collected and stored, and the potential problems inherent in its misuse, have led to the introduction of legislation designed to prevent abuse and to place restrictions on its use.

Over 30 countries have now enacted privacy and data protection laws, for example the Privacy and Privacy Protection Acts of 1974 and 1980 respectively in the United States, and the 1984 Data Protection Act in the United Kingdom. In Europe, this tends to take the form of so-called 'omnibus legislation', aimed at say the protection of all data in whatever form, rather than at, for example, banking privacy. In the United States, on the other hand, where the issue tends to be known as 'fair information practice', a piecemeal approach has been preferred. The main explanation for this difference in response lies in an American reluctance to overlegislate on this issue for fear of possible repercussions on trade. These fears are far from groundless and reflect both the dual nature of this privacy issue and the change which has overtaken it. Hence, what began as a concern for personal privacy became entangled with the commercial aspects of data protection, with the whole affair burgeoning into an international issue over transborder dataflows.

Major considerations in the field of privacy legislation include the issues of 'legal persons' and control mechanisms. The former concerns whether privacy rights should extend to companies and other corporate bodies or refer only to private individuals. The latter issue is to do with the ultimate authority in such matters, and with whether the Courts, an ombudsman system or some alternative arrangement would be best suited to effecting the oversight of data protection activity. Existing legislation applies to both public and private databanks. It not only imposes restrictions on the use of such data by those who collect it, and by third parties, but also requires rights of access and correction for the data subjects, the real 'owners' of the information. Many countries have created national bodies specifically to oversee this legislation and, in a number of cases, the list of possible sanctions includes imprisonment.[13]

Furthermore, with data processing increasingly linked to considerations of political sovereignty, there has been a tendency towards internationalisation of the apparatus of control, notably through such bodies as the OECD and the Council of Europe. As its name implies, the *OECD guidelines governing the protection of privacy and transborder flows of personal data* provides a standard to be aimed for, rather than a legal requirement. However, its basic principles of care in the collection and use of personal data, with appropriate safeguards for the rights of the data subject, have found general acceptability, with the Irish Republic the only member of the OECD to withhold its consent.[13] The Council of Europe's *Convention for the protection of individuals with regard to automatic processing of data* is a much more stringent document. It carries the strength of an international treaty and requires its signatories to enact legislation to implement its recommendations. Like the OECD guidelines, it came into force during 1985.

Freedom of information

There is a clear connection between freedom of information and privacy, essentially as reflected in the need to balance access to information with the right to privacy. The concept of freedom of information is based upon the premise that, in a democracy, the citizen should have reasonable access to information, particularly government information, except where there are security or similar considerations to be taken into account. Nevertheless, in the United Kingdom, where there is no guarantee of this access, it is precisely such reasonable-sounding premises as the need for security, and protection of the wider public interest, that have so far negated a long-running and determined 'Freedom of Information' campaign. In the United Kingdom, the major legislative obstacle to the wider dissemination of information held secretly in public sources is Section 2 of the Official Secrets Act, 1911. In relation to much of the information thus locked away from public view, implementation of this Act is very much akin to taking a sledgehammer to crack a nut.

In the United States, where there is freedom of information legislation, they have a relatively open approach to this question of information access. Generally speaking, information created or collected by the government is available, unless limited by national security considerations or to prevent disclosure of personal data provided by private citizens to government agencies. Although one of the recurring objections to the enactment of such legislation is that of the supposed cost to the national exchequer, it is interesting to note that in the American experience this has worked out at less than the cost of maintaining golf courses for service personnel serving overseas.

It seems ironic that in a country with such a long-standing tradition of parliamentary democracy as the United Kingdom, there is still no legislation relating to freedom of information. Indeed, while the issue has been around for at least 15 years, and despite statements of intent by both Conservative and Labour administrations, the matter seems as far away from resolution as ever. In fact, no less a person than Mrs Thatcher has defended the adequacy of existing arrangements, arguing that a statutory right of public access to government information would erode the principle of ministerial accountability to Parliament, and thus diminish the authority of Parliament itself.[14] Nonetheless, the 'Freedom of Information' campaign shows little sign of flagging in its efforts to secure not just access to government and official information, but also individual privacy rights in information, and the repeal of the Official Secrets Act. Launched in 1984, and directed by Mr Des Wilson, it has all-party support and considerable backing outside Parliament.[14]

Support for the principle of information access has been forthcoming at the international level as well, notably within the Council of Europe. There, the Council of Ministers has launched a review of Article 10 of the European Convention on Human Rights, with a view to extending freedom of information to those countries which still refuse to enact national legislation in this regard. It is worth pointing out, however, that in places such as Australia and the United States there has been something of a 'backlash' against existing freedom of information practices. In some instances this is a reaction to security leaks or to the transfer of strategically important technology to potential enemy countries. In others it is based on suspicions that the freedom of information concerned is often enjoyed more by the media and by business organisations than by the individual citizen, and employed either to embarass the government of the day or to obtain some kind of commercial advantage.[15] Nevertheless, such abuses, or potential abuses, would seem to be part of the price paid for living in an open society, where in any event occasional instances of government discomfort may well contribute to the general good. In the United Kingdom many of the activities liable to prosecution under the Official Secrets Act are innocuous indeed, while serious breaches of national security continue to occur despite the operation of the Act. It is clearly time for new legislation to be enacted. In any case, the United Kingdom may well find itself overtaken by events and required to fall into line with freedom of information regulations laid down elsewhere, for example within the European Community.

Computer crime

Computer crime is now assuming such proportions that it could well become the subject of a major OECD enquiry. As with so many of the issues discussed in this chapter, this is in essence a legal matter, one which involves the definition of theft. Where, hitherto, theft was defined as some variation of the unlawful removal of somebody else's goods or property, the position is no longer quite so clearcut. With the automation of data, and its storage and retrieval using computers, simple access to information can be all that is required for the law to be broken. More complex versions of this computer crime are the result of actual interference with automated information, or its deliberate corruption or manipulation for some unlawful purpose. What is more, although the practice of unauthorised intrusion into somebody else's computer files has added the word 'hacker' to the English language, the problem is frequently one of criminal behaviour on the part of authorised and otherwise legitimate users. Finally, like the systems upon which it is based, computer crime knows no national borders, and as a result can be extremely difficult to detect. It is bound to have the most far-reaching implications for the legal system, both at national and international level.

Intellectual property

A fundamental difficulty facing current attempts to cope with matters of data security and computer crime is the inadequacy of legal provision in such matters. To an extent this has to do with the nature of information itself, and with the difficulties of arriving at a single, coherent concept which can then be defended. To date, the law has defined information in terms of 'intellectual property', with ownership of the idea or knowledge concerned being invested in the person who produced it. However, if ownership of information is implicitly vested in the person who generated the idea, then consider the implications when this knowledge is subsequently embedded into a particular media format, for example an online database. What is needed, therefore, is a new statutory definition of property to encompass information, particularly new information held in electronic form.[15]

Something of the complexity of this legal situation can be inferred from the need for reforms, not just in specific areas like electronic funds transfer but also, in fact, in such fundamental branches of the law as contract and evidence. At an international level, moreover, there is the thorny question of jurisdiction, that is: where breaches of intellectual property law have been committed, involving people in a number of countries, according to whose laws will the case be tried?

More optimistically, it is possible that the very technology which creates these problems – by making the theft of intellectual property such a simple matter – could itself provide the answer. While legal sanctions might be available, the real answer could lie in protection by such devices as encryption. Encryption, involving digital 'signatures' for authorised users, and separate keys for enciphering and for deciphering messages, has the particular advantage that even if an intruder gains access to the system the data is still secure.[16]

Vulnerability

Serious as it is, the problem of computer-related crime is itself only part of a potentially much greater problem. The more that society comes to rely upon technology, the more vulnerable it becomes to the possibility of some form of technological breakdown. Nowhere is this vulnerability more apparent than in the case of computers, which play a key role in just about every major administrative and technical operation performed today. Imagine the chaos that would result from a failure of the computers employed in air traffic control or in the social security system. Imagine what would happen following breakdown of those international networks upon which banks, airlines, multinational corporations and, indeed, governments have come to depend. The vulnerability of society to such threats is a matter for consideration at the highest international levels.

In Sweden the Sark Report has called for legal rather than administrative measures to guard against such eventualities.[17] This report identified the most likely sources of damage to electronic data as operator error, accident, natural disaster, acts of terrorism, industrial action, and political or industrial espionage. Improbable as some of these might sound, the susceptibility of computerised data to damage or unlawful interference requires that every eventuality be considered in drawing up protective measures. By the same token, there has to be a balance drawn between the operation of sensible security controls and the avoidance of oppressive and ultimately self-defeating approaches to this very important issue.

Alienation

As employed here, alienation denotes a feeling of separation from society. It is a sense of being left behind by developments which, in effect, take on overtones of domination of the individual by the system. In view of all that has been said about the enabling power of the new technology, its transforming and at times revolutionary nature, it is not difficult to draw the connection between IT and alienation in modern societies. Nor is this simply a matter of theoretical observation. The European Community's FAST programme has identified as a strategic issue the matter of alienation or integration of the individual and of groups in an information society.[18]

Unemployment is an obvious source of potential alienation and again has become the focus of European concern. The Commission of the European Communities has devised strategies to deal with, for example, the impact of microelectronics on unemployment, and to help both society and industry master the new technologies and adapt to their use.[18] The importance of such action programmes can be seen in the incipient alienation among the young unemployed in many inner city areas of the world. Likewise, continuing difficulties over problems of data protection and privacy suggest that there are few grounds for complacency. Even Masuda has admitted the possibility of life lived in a future automated state, a horrible and forbidding age.[19] This much said, however, information technology is likely to create just as many jobs as it is claimed to destroy, and by the same token it cannot be made the sole scapegoat for alienation. Nevertheless, the subject of alienation is a serious one and should be treated accordingly. In terms of technology and its social impact, this entails a need to educate and to explain. Governments must acknowledge the fears of ordinary people in respect of new technology and the information society. They must listen rather than simply go on extolling the virtues of such developments.

References

1. Cronin, Blaise, The information society, *Aslib Proceedings*, 38, 4, April 1986, 121–29.
2. Brimmer, Carl W., U.S. telecommunications common carrier policy, in *Annual review of information science & technology*, vol. 17, ed. M. E. Williams, White Plains, New York, Knowledge Industry Publications, 1982, 33–82.

3. Flowerdew, A. D. C. et al., *The pricing and provision of information*, London, British Library, 1984. (R&D Report 20.)

4. The sleeping giant, *The Economist*, 23 April 1983, 16–17.

5. Brimmer, op. cit., 53.

6. Cawkell, Anthony E., ed., *Handbook of information technology and office systems*, Amsterdam, North Holland, 1986, 66.

7. Flowerdew et al., op. cit., 30.

8. Masuda, Yoneji, Computopia, in *The information technology revolution*, ed. Tom Forrester, Oxford, Blackwell, 1985, 620–35.

9. Robbins, Kevin, New technology: the political economy of General Ludd, in *Information technology: impact on the way of life*, vol. 2, Dublin, National Board for Science & Technology, 1981, Conference preprints.

10. Garnham, Nicolas, The information society is also a class society, in *Information technology: impact on the way of life*, vol. 2, Conference preprints.

11. Schiller, Herbert, *Who knows: information in the age of the Fortune 500*, Norwood, New Jersey, Ablex, 1985, 55.

12. Cullen, John, Impact of information technology on human wellbeing, in *Information technology: impact on the way of life*, vol. 2, Conference preprints.

13. Sutherland, Ewan, ed., 'Telecommunications: policy issues and regulatory practices affecting the future', Proceedings of the Salzburg Seminar, 1985, Session 243, Unpublished.

14. *The U.K. information industry: current issues. Public rights of access to information*, Fact sheet, 9, London, British Library, 1985.

15. Sutherland, op. cit., 26.

16. *The U.K. information industry: current issues. Computer security*, Fact sheet, 7, London, British Library, 1985.

17. Sutherland, op. cit., 27.

18. Grewlich, Klaus and Finn Pedersen, eds., *Power and participation in an information society*, Luxembourg, Commission of the European Communities, 1984.

19. Masuda, op. cit., 629.

CHAPTER 6

The economics of the information society

Any attempt to understand the workings of the information society will of necessity include some overview of the economic factors involved. The objective will be to adhere to the broad principles of economic science while putting forward the complementary and overlapping economic perspectives of certain other disciplines with an interest in the information society.

It should be made clear that economists have always been interested in information, which in fact is central to the study of microeconomics – the economics of households, firms and markets. During the 1960s, people such as Machlup and Lamberton began to explore the wider, sectoral implications of information, with growing evidence of structural economic change linked to an emerging apparatus of technology. They were joined during the 1970s by a group of information scientists interested primarily in the cost and value aspects of information and its related systems – in what in many respects was the economics of the information industry. This industry emerged with the revolution in information technologies, which created a range of entirely different information goods and services. It is given separate treatment in the following chapter.

In this chapter the objective is to cover the broad field of information economics, lest an overemphasis on information sectors or on systems and services obscure the pervasive importance of information in other markets.[1] The underlying thesis will be that two sets of changes have occurred within the field of information economics. The first has been an increased awareness of the importance of information as a resource in its own right. The second has involved the growth of interest in the role of information in advanced economies, a role deemed by many to be decisive. Information societies, the argument goes, are also information economies.

The economic characteristics of information

These changes notwithstanding, it would seem fair to say that the response of the economics profession as a whole to such developments has been somewhat muted. A possible explanation could lie in an understandable reluctance on the part of many economists to perceive information as being somehow different, a factor deserving of special treatment. In fact, information shares common characteristics with a number of other factors in that it can be bought and sold, and is a source of added value, of market power and of uncertainty. On the other hand, information has certain more individual characteristics, including difficulties relating to its measurement and the presence of so-called externalities. These characteristics are now considered briefly in turn.

Not a free good

Traditionally economists and others have treated information as an overhead, as something which could be taken for granted, as a given. These attitudes can be explained partly by a concern for equity, for example the desire to defend the principle of free access to information through the provision of a public library service. In part, too, the explanation lies in the practical difficulties involved in attempting to separate information costs from other costs. However, a growing awareness of the resource characteristics of information, the emergence of markets for information goods and services, and the continuing need for financial accountability and control have gradually eroded both traditional attitudes and established practices.

Perhaps the most significant breakthrough has come with the realisation, now widespread, that information is not a free good. There are costs associated with its production, distribution and exchange, and the fact that these have been borne by either the public or the corporate purse makes them no less real. Therefore, while different in some respects from other commodities, information shares the common economic characteristics of having exchange value on the market. As with other marketable resources, moreover, information can be both a consumption good and an investment good. As a consumption good, information itself is the end product or service being offered. As an investment good, it contributes at an intermediate stage to the production of other goods and services. In either case information costs money and is definitely not to be treated as a free good.

A source of added value

One of the more obvious illustrations of the economic nature of information lies in its relation to the concept of added value. Information can add value to other factors and processes and can itself be enhanced in value through additional inputs of information. Relevant or up-to-date information can clearly make a difference to the competitive position of any company. Similarly, the refinement or repackaging of information by brokers or other intermediaries is a growing source of added value. This helps to emphasise another important aspect of information, that frequently the exploitation of one category depends upon being able to combine it with other categories of information.

A source of market power

Another important characteristic of information, especially in view of its key role in the market system, is that it affords various possibilities for market power. Whereas in an ideal market all players are price takers, with no individual buyer or seller having market power – that is the power to affect price or supply significantly – actual markets for information contain monopoly elements. These monopoly elements can take a variety of forms, and those most likely to arise where information is concerned are the so-called natural monopolies. A natural monopoly is one brought about either by scale or by the action of government. In terms of scale, a natural monopoly exists where any one firm or combination of firms produces so large a proportion of the total output of a commodity that it can raise price by restricting output.[2] In the case of the information industry it is not too difficult to envisage this kind of situation developing with regard to those major multinational companies which enjoy dominant positions in entire areas of both equipment production and service provision.

So far as government-induced monopolies are concerned, the classic example has long been that of telecommunications services, although the onset of deregulation has tended to complicate the position in that industry. Another long-standing example of government-induced monopoly is the practice of granting patents and copyrights to the creators of new information by, in effect, recognising ownership in what is termed intellectual property. All such monopolies require some form of government regulation to prevent abuse of their market power. Their ultimate justification is on grounds of economies of scale and of benefits to the consumer.

Information and uncertainty

All markets are prey to uncertainties, a future which is best understood in terms of the more familiar concept of risk. Uncertainty refers to the kind of risk – say changes in demand or in the level of competition – against which it is impossible to take out insurance, as compared to such insurable risks as fire or theft.[3] In the case of those information markets where what is for sale is not an information product but judgement or experience, uncertainty can be a particular problem. While actual sight of the information might dispel client uncertainty as to its usefulness, it could also obviate the need to spend any more money on the service.

Uncertainties can arise at both the stage of production and at the point of exchange, and for present purposes they provide an excellent example of the essential unity of information economics. The market is, in effect, a kind of information system designed to bring together people with complementary wants, namely a desire to trade. However, this system is by no means perfect and, owing to information asymmetries, not all buyers and sellers are equally well informed. Therefore, in all markets, and not just those for information goods and services, the link between information and uncertainty is a key influence on market structure and operation.[4] Put differently, this means that the distorting effects of these gaps in information provision serve to emphasise the continued importance of information economics.

Externalities

More peculiarly a characteristic of information is the presence of externalities. Externalities, or external economies, are defined as favourable effects on one or more persons that come from the action of a different person or firm. Negative externalities, or external diseconomies, occur in the same fashion, except that they refer to harm done to others from an external source. Externalities are notable features of what are known as public or social goods. With public goods, if one person has more there is no reduction in the quantity available for everybody else. In the case of information, this entails the characteristic of durability. This means that the resource is not depleted as it is consumed, whereas a private good, say a bar of chocolate, once eaten, is used up, leaving nothing for anyone else. Lighthouses and defence are the classic examples of public goods, because it is as easy to provide these services to everybody as to a few people. They would also be unattractive prospects for private enterprise.[5]

With information, certain difficulties arise from the existence of these externalities. In the matter of ownership, for example, there is a strong negative externality in the fact that, frequently, ownership rights in information simply cannot be enforced. Further difficulties arise from the characteristics of nonrivalry and nonexclusiveness in consumption. Nonrivalry means that additional users can be supplied at zero cost without reducing the benefits to existing users. Nonexclusiveness means that no matter how many users are involved they cannot be excluded from using the information. Thus, given the impracticality of charging for such use, and the inability to exclude nonpayers, a private market will often not be possible.[6] A final example of information externalities is that arising from the distribution effects of information transfer. In this case the adoption of more efficient manufacturing techniques, the substitution of one product or service for another, or simply the acquisition by an individual of a certain piece of information can lead to changes in income distribution and wealth. Of course, these distribution effects, or pecuniary externalities, can work in both directions, leaving people either richer or poorer.

Uncertainties in return

Reference has already been made to the public goods characteristics of information, and to the link between information and uncertainty. Many in the information community would take this public goods aspect as evidence of the inherently beneficial qualities of information, which, in principle as well as in practice, they are bound to promote. Thus, where many noneconomists would welcome as a matter of course the possibility of increased investment in, say, education or research, some economists at least could be expected to scrutinise such proposals from a public interest standpoint, not least because of the presence of uncertainties.

This illustrates an important difference in attitudes towards information, and introduces one of its final characteristics. In the case of pecuniary externalities, there can be a discrepancy between the benefit that accrues to society and that accruing to the individual researcher or the owner of the data. In such cases it is not that the public goods characteristics of the resulting information are impaired, but rather that the private return on the public investment in education or research exceeds the social return. The uncertainties involved concern both the most likely beneficiaries of public expenditure and the desirability of undertaking the original investment. This question of private versus social return is one which occurs throughout the field of information economics.

The problem of measurement

A continued source of weakness in the study of information economics is the absence of reliable measures for such fundamental elements as cost, price and value. This situation can be exacerbated by the diverging interpretations placed upon such concepts by the different disciplines involved. A brief consideration of each of these elements in turn should help to illustrate the more obvious effects of this measurement problem.

Cost. While cost is a familiar and, apparently, obvious concept, it is in fact a highly ambiguous one, and capable of a range of interpretations. When noneconomists use the term, they are generally referring to monetary costs, whereas economists would include consideration of opportunity costs. Opportunity cost represents the cost of forgone alternatives, the need to satisfy one want at the sacrifice of another, say forgoing the chance of a holiday abroad in order to purchase a motor car.

In addition to differences in interpretation, the measurement of costs can be complicated by the difficulties of separating information costs from other costs. While real enough, it can be easy to overstate such difficulties, however, and given an existing ability to distinguish, for example, materials costs from personnel costs, or to separate online charges from those for hardware or software, a fair amount of cost analysis for information can be carried out. Viewed from the alternative angle of justification, moreover, the material may be ephemeral or long-lasting, highly specialised or widely applicable, costly or cheap to produce. Not infrequently, however, the problem, where it exists, has been one of reporting procedures, and with the emergence of specialised budgetary and accounting techniques for information management there is clear scope for improvement. One thing is quite certain, however, and that is that information costs can no longer simply be imputed or set aside as unimportant.

Price. In conceptual terms, price can be compared with cost in that it too can be seen in the context of something forgone in order to obtain something else. Price is usually denoted in monetary terms, as the amount of money that has to be paid in order to obtain a good or a service, but it need not necessarily be in monetary form. Price is related to cost, both on the theoretical level and in the context of the market, most notably in the matter of cost recovery.

Strategies for cost recovery will vary with the immediate objectives of the company and, especially, with whether the aim is to cover all costs, to cover some costs only, or to make a profit. Depending on these objectives, a firm may decide to aim for either marginal cost pricing or average cost pricing. With marginal cost pricing, the price is set at the margin – the cost associated with each additional unit of a product or each extra use of a service. Thus, under conditions of perfect competition, price equals marginal cost, and profits will be maximised. In the real world, however, ideal conditions seldom apply, and marginal costing may well be suboptimal. Often in practice, the price is set at a level equal to the average cost per item sold or service provided. Price can also be set at a level somewhere above that, depending on what the market will bear. This latter example shows that, under appropriate conditions, the pricing of information goods and services occurs in a manner very much akin to that for other commodities. This is clearly borne out by the experience of the online information industry.

Value. The question of information value is a complex matter, and one which lies at the heart of information economics. Moreover, few aspects of this developing subject are more vulnerable to subjective judgement, as can be seen in the continuing debate over whether information should be free as of right to all who require it, or made available on the basis of payment.

As with the matter of costs, the economists have introduced an additional nonmonetary dimension to the assessment of information value. While recognising that, as defined in monetary terms, the value of a good or service determines its price, economists since the eighteenth century have distinguished between value in exchange and value in use. This concern with utility, the capacity to satisfy human needs, was refined by the neoclassical economists to the point where the theory of value became one of the allocation of scarce resources, with marginal utility a key determinant of market price. In modern economics, the prices of goods, that is value in exchange, are usually taken as determined by the interaction of a set of demand curves with a set of supply curves. Each demand curve is the aggregation of the individual demand curves for that commodity, each based on utility maximisation, and each supply curve is similarly based on individual producer profit maximisation behaviour.

Clearly, the question of value in information is one which noneconomists should approach with care. Even where a broader view is taken, moreover, the problems of measurement remain. Thus, while in one sense value can be measured by what a person is prepared to pay for some good or service, in another sense it is based on future expectations, and these are not easily susceptible of measurement.[7] Attempts to circumvent this difficulty by means of cost-benefit analysis encounter similar problems of the assignment of monetary values to variables.[7] Nonetheless, the fact that these problems of measurement are now much more widely appreciated is in itself a positive development.

Information and markets

In bringing this first section of the chapter to a close, let us re-emphasise the centrality of information to the study of economics, and its specific implications for the economics of information. In making this general point, Spence has emphasised the critical importance of such information-intensive behaviour as searching and signalling.[8] Searching can be thought of as a process by which agents in the economic process acquire information. The problems they face in this regard are little different in their essentials from other kinds of information retrieval problems. Signals are the means by which people on either side of the market – buyers and sellers – transmit information to each other.

Signalling is something that happens in all markets, and its importance can be underlined with respect to two particular fields: the job market and advertising. In the job market context, there is a particularly full range of signals, with educational qualifications and employment history seen as among the most effective means of conveying information about prospective employees. This too is a complex process, with indications that employers in fact send out their own signals in order to induce would-be employees to structure their signals in a way likely to convey more meaningful information about themselves to the companies.[8] There is a strong similarity between this type of activity and the structural theories of information behaviour encountered in Chapter 1.

Just as the job applicant sends out a stream of signals designed to convey the right kind of information to potential employers, so the advertising agencies direct their own information signals at prospective customers. In neither case can the intended receivers be sure that the information they are receiving is correct, although the advertising industry is particularly vulnerable to credibility problems. This is owing to both the commercial nature of the transaction and the fact that it actually involves an attempt to influence consumer behaviour. Its major difficulties lie in what have been labelled the 'experience qualities' of goods or services, that is in providing the kind of information that will induce people to spend money on goods or services whose utility or quality will not be revealed until after they have acquired them. Apart from the making of fraudulent claims, which can be an expensive and ultimately self-defeating business, the main means of overcoming this problem is to seek credibility through the establishment of brand names in which the public will have confidence. As Spence points out, however, the establishment of brand names can itself affect the efficiency of the market by resulting in a form of monopolistic competition, with consumers opting for the familiar product or service as against the new arrival.[8] Common to all these activities, however, and as much a part of mainstream economic activity as is that branch which has come to bear its name, is the information factor.

Economics: macro and micro

In considering the major economic characteristics of information, the focus so far has been on the narrower, more detailed aspects of the subject, on the microeconomics of information. This has been necessary for some kind of an understanding of information markets, and of the forces which operate within them. The broader aspect of economics is concerned with the national or macro level. The macroeconomics of information is, therefore, the study of information within the national economy, its impact upon, and implications for, growth, output and employment, productivity and economic policy. If the key areas of microeconomics as applied to information are those of cost, price and value, then the equivalent concerns at the macro level are the information economy and policies appropriate to its development.

The information economy

Bearing in mind that economists have been familiar with the concept for at least 20 years, it seems reasonable to ask why the information economy has not attracted more interest in economics circles. One explanation could be that noneconomists have overreacted to something which is not really all that significant. Further reasons could include differing perspectives on information, on the economic aggregates involved, and even on whether this is properly a matter for economists in the first place.

As stated, the thesis is comparatively simple. Analogous to the Agricultural and Industrial revolutions of earlier centuries, a further shift of economic activity has occurred, based this time upon the information resource. Overshadowing traditional factors of production such as land, labour and capital, this information factor increasingly holds the key to growth, output and employment. Furthermore, advanced countries today are evolving as information economies, ever more dependent upon a range of knowledge-intensive information goods and services.

Measuring the information economy

Despite a fair amount of work in this area, there is still a problem of quantification where the information economy is concerned. Essentially the difficulty is one of classification, and of the need to disaggregate existing statistical series in order to isolate the information components. Among attempts to classify information activities for purposes of measurement, those of Machlup and Porat stand out as seminal contributions. In his pioneering analysis of the US National Income Accounts, Machlup depicted economic activity in terms of those establishments that produced knowledge and information goods and services, either for their own use or for use by others. To this end, he devised a basic typology of information activities, which included education, research and development, media of communication, information machinery, and information services.[9] Although criticised for its all-inclusiveness, Machlup's methodology paved the way for a thorough investigation of the nature and characteristics of information, and of its role in economic affairs. Inevitably, both the concept itself and the terminology employed were much amended by subsequent researchers, often with confusing consequences.

Foremost among Machlup's successors was Marc Porat, whose work for the United States Department of Commerce in 1978 was destined to reach a much wider audience. Using the same data, Porat expanded Machlup's typology into two information sectors, the one primary, the other secondary. The Primary Information Sector (PIS) included all those goods and services which intrinsically conveyed information, such as books, or which were directly useful in its production, processing or distribution, such as computers.[10] Significantly, in order to be included in the PIS, these goods and services normally had to be transacted on established markets. In essence, therefore, the PIS was the productive locus of an information-based economy, including both the technological infrastructure for information processing and transmission, and the actual market transactions.[11]

Porat realised, however, that a large number of information transactions were in fact carried on inside organisations and thus outside the market. In order to account for such activity, Porat devised his Secondary Information Sector (SIS), which included all those information activities involved in the production of noninformation goods and services, and not traded on the market. Into this SIS, therefore, would fall the activities of, for example, in-house prin'ing or accounting departments in companies whose primary concern was with the manufacture of something else, say aircraft or food products. According to Porat's calculations, the PIS and SIS together accounted for 46 per cent of the United States GNP in 1966, a figure later revised by Oettinger to 54 per cent for 1980.[12]

In constructing this SIS, Porat sought to eliminate the undercounting of information activities in the economy. It is now widely accepted that somewhere between 50 and 60 per cent of the GNPs of the member states of the OECD can be ascribed to activity within his two sectors. The most recent information available, which updates an OECD study conducted in 1981, reveals that although in both cases the growth rate has slowed down, the share of information occupations in the labour force, and that of information goods and services in national incomes, has continued to rise.[12] This is broadly in line with the findings of the 1985 study undertaken in the United Kingdom by the Technical Change Centre (TCC), which introduced, as a refinement of the sectoral approach, the 'Information Complex'.[13] A mixture of sectors, occupations, technologies and the producers and users of information goods and services, this also incorporated a novel variant of the traditional dichotomy between goods and services, as devised by ITAP. Analogous to the distinction between ends and means, to the standard goods and services division were added the dimensions of 'content' and 'enabling', producing, in effect, four sub-sectors. These were product content sectors, such as publishing; product enabling sectors, such as computing equipment; service content sectors, such as brokerages; and service enabling sectors, such as telecommunications.[13] Sectoral studies of this kind can help to build up a deeper understanding of the information economy, although difficulties remain. Before turning to some of these problem areas, it will first be necessary to consider the key components of this information economy.

Components of the information economy

Although there is a reasonable consensus as to what would be contained within the broad spectrum of the information economy or, more narrowly, in an information sector, there continues to be lively discussion at the detailed level. Among the major foci of debate are the information workforce, information goods and services, information markets, and the information infrastructure.

Information workforce

Whereas until fairly recently the designation of information worker would have applied most comfortably to a coherent group of occupations within the library and information science field, the term has now acquired a much wider connotation. Clearly, those statistics which indicate that over half the labour force in advanced economies is engaged in information work[11] are concerned not with what might be termed the 'core' of traditional information professions, but with a much larger grouping of information-related occupations. Viewed as those occupations whose primary purpose is an output of produced, processed or distributed information, or its infrastructure support, the concept of an information workforce becomes more tenable. Within this workforce are grouped occupations whose output has value because of its information content, as in, for example, a memorandum, a decision or a research report, rather than because of its physical content, as in, say, a motor car or a piece of furniture. Information workers are engaged in the creation and processing of knowledge, and in the manipulation of symbols, rather than in the physical handling of goods or material services.

Current typologies of information occupations are strongly influenced by the earlier efforts of Machlup and Porat. In the event, these reflect a tendency to be overinclusive and thus to inflate the size of the information workforce. Nevertheless, the problem does seem to have settled down to one of individual job classifications, with the broad outlines of these classifications acceptable to a growing constituency. As a result, the major groupings of information occupations emerge as in Table 2.

These categories have been revised by the TCC for its own classification of information occupations.[15] However, the underlying construct of a group of information-related occupations, of an information workforce, remains the same. Although, in practice, these typologies will provoke questions as to the primary function of, say, judges, medical doctors and dentists, who are

Table 2. Information occupations

Information producers	Create new information or package existing information into more appropriate form.
Information processors	Receive and respond to information inputs as the basis for further action.
Information distributors	Convey information from the initiator to the recipient.
Information infrastructure	Installation, operation and repair of the machines and technologies used to support information activities.[14]

frequently classified as providers of private information services, they serve as useful tools for the analysis of the information workforce. It is to be hoped that, in illustrating the changing nature of information work, these classifications will also shed light on the development of information economies.

Information goods and services

Clearly, the same contextual and classificatory conditions apply to all the likely components of the information economy. As for information goods and services, these have tended to find acceptance through repetition and use, rather than by conscious efforts at classification. Nevertheless, a certain amount of awareness will have been fostered by the development of goods and services typologies. Within such typologies, information goods tend to include such items as office, computing and accounting machines; radio, television and communications equipment; and books and magazines. Information services, on the other hand, range over such activities as education; research and development; computer processing; data communications; and myriad business, financial, legal and management services.

An additional characteristic of these information goods and services is that, frequently, they are updated versions of more familiar products or services. Examples include the designation of objects such as books or telephones as information products and the reclassification of such everyday facilities as travel agencies or government services as informational. At a different level, there has been the development of completely new information products such as microcomputers or video recorders, or the provision of completely new information services based on the converging technologies of computing and telecommunications.

Advances in information technology have not just enabled certain functions to be performed faster, more cheaply and more effectively, but also created new ways of doing things, new products and new services. In such a context, there is definite validity in Porat's description of information goods and services as those which intrinsically convey information or which are directly useful in its production, processing or distribution. As products, they can take the form of both capital and consumption goods: the former including, say, digitally controlled machine tools or word processors; the latter, home computers or cellular telephones. As services, they can appear in familiar guise as libraries or news agencies, or more innovatively as online information services, computer-based messaging or electronic funds transfer.

Information markets

As Porat has pointed out, the true significance of these phenomena is as neither goods nor services, nor as isolated activities, but as a coherent information market.[16] Information markets are created when a technology of information production and distribution is organised by firms, and an exchange price established.[16] These markets first emerged in countries with a highly developed services sector and sufficient local demand to support an indigenous information industry. However, for reasons of both scale and profit, they have outgrown national boundaries and the information industry is now a truly international affair. These international markets are fiercely contested and the players involved seem condemned to re-learning all the hard-won lessons of earlier days in regard to protectionism, tariff wars and similar barriers to trade. Nevertheless, the information marketplace is already of such significance as to be the object of attention not just from commercial organisations but also from national and international governments. It is in such markets that many of the hopes for growth and employment in the foreseeable future reside.

Information infrastructure

The infrastructure element of the information economy is perhaps the least contentious of all its components, if only because it is an accepted part of the traditional economic infrastructure. Included in the infrastructure of an information economy, therefore, would be such familiar elements as education and training; research and development; media of communication;

telecommunications; and such support facilities as grants and incentives, advisory services and technical assistance.

Two points in particular need to be emphasised about the contents of this infrastructure. The first concerns the importance of education and training – something that is likely to become even more critical in future information-based economies. This is because an educated and adaptable population will be needed not only to provide the kind of workforce required but also as a source of demand for the output of the information industry.[17] The second point concerns the importance of telecommunications, which, apart from being part of that essential infrastructure upon which modern industry depends, is a key growth point for future economic activity. Indeed, the telecommunications network is already being hailed as the infrastructure for the coming information society, a claim which appears less futuristic when set against the emergence of a worldwide information trade operating in a so-called 'network marketplace'.

A critical perspective on the information economy

Seen from a certain perspective, publication of the TCC report was but further confirmation, if any were needed, of the advent in the United Kingdom of a new kind of economy – an information economy. What was happening marked not just the emergence of services as the dominant sector in the economy but also the fact that the fastest-growing elements in this sector were services with a high information content. Moreover, this was merely a repetition of the experience of the United States, where, it is reported, information workers now comprise a majority of the labour force.[18] Seen from a different perspective, however, matters are by no means so clear cut.

To begin with, there are still fundamental difficulties to do with measurement. All major studies to date have drawn liberally on such standard statistical sources as national income accounts and national and international classifications of industries and occupations, all of which largely ignore the information variable. Clearly, researchers can work only with the tools at their disposal and, in criticising such efforts, there is always a danger of overemphasising the details of the methodology at the expense of that which is being counted. Nevertheless, the fact that this entire edifice of information economics rests upon a reworking of figures drawn from different national series and compiled for completely different purposes must inevitably raise questions of accuracy and reliability.

There is also a fair measure of confusion over the real nature of these developments. That structural change has taken place is quite obvious. What is much less clear is whether this process, which is still under way, is occurring throughout the economy or within certain relatively discrete sectors. In a sense, the distinction is academic or at most terminological, with the issue being one of nomenclature, that of information economy versus information sector. Hence, if an information sector is emerging as a wealth-creating enclave within the economy, as an engine of growth, then for all practical purposes this reflects the advent of an information economy. But is this what is actually happening? There is a strong body of opinion which holds that what is occurring is not informational at all but is related to the development of services. Thus, it is argued, relative shifts in factor prices, themselves the result of productivity improvements and the widespread application of new technologies, reflect the emergence of services as the major source of income and employment within modern economies. Hence, runs the argument, the focus of attention should be on services rather than on spurious information entities, which are simply the outcome of re-labelling exercises.

Turning to the occupational component, a key element in either side of the argument, there is indeed evidence of what could be termed 're-labelling'. Many familiar, even mundane, occupations have been designated as informational, often it would seem on somewhat tenuous grounds. The basis for such activity has been the principle of 'primary purpose', in that it is those occupations whose primary purpose involves an output of produced, processed or distributed information that are designated as information activities. Plausible as this might sound, its application in practice has led to some rather peculiar instances of classification. Thus, one would argue, doctors heal the sick, estate agents sell property and whereas both teachers and lawyers are in fact creators and users of information, it remains at least debatable as to whether their primary purpose is informational. Similar objections can be raised as to the information credentials of such 'blue chip' members of the tradeable information establishment as banking and financial services, and this despite their commitment to the use of advanced information technologies. Individual examples aside, however, it is on the credibility of such classificatory activity that the case for the information economy stands or falls. If key occupational areas were excluded from consideration, then the knock-on effect in both quantitative and qualitative terms would be considerable.

There is, of course, another side to the story. In many cases there is much more to these occupations than simply white collar work and the absence of a tangible end product. The services themselves need first to be disaggregated into information services and other services, for example online information provision or business consultancy, as opposed to hairdressing or window-cleaning. Moreover, many of the industries and services classed as informational are in fact heavily knowledge-intensive. This can be seen from the presence of such factor inputs as qualified personnel, large amounts of research and development and advanced information technologies. There is also the value-added character of many such services, whose essential impetus derives directly from exploiting the commercial potential of the information resource and its associated technologies. Finally, there is the fact of government interest all over the world in the growth-inducing potential of these information activities. Whether it be the Alvey Programme in the United Kingdom, the Brazilian Government's national informatics plans, or the proposals for development of a single market for the European information industry, there is clearly more to such activities than can be explained by a propensity to re-label things.

Information in the economy

This chapter has attempted to provide something of the economic background to those wider changes which are affecting societies all over the world. In arguing for the indivisibility of the two major variables, it has tried to demonstrate the central importance of the economics of information to the overall processes of change and development. Although on occasions economists and noneconomists appear to have taken distinctly different approaches to the subject, there has long been an element of cooperation between the two, and there is mutual advantage to this being increased. Non-economists have clearly much to learn from the economics profession in relation to information behaviour and the wider implications of market structure and operation. At the macro level, also, there is a clear need for the added rigour of formal economic science, although growing interest in the notion of information-based economies suggests that the flow of ideas has not been entirely unidirectional.

As for the information economy, a concept especially germane to the present volume, the evidence remains as inconclusive and as tied to subjective perceptions as ever. Thus, on the one hand, a recent OECD paper stated categorically that the term 'information economy' was employed not because of any distinct socioeconomic significance but because it was clearly understandable in the context of the programme in question.[19] On the other hand, it reported the continued growth of both information-related income and employment. Even more significant, however, is a suggestion that, as reflected in the percentage share of information occupations in the labour force of six of the nine OECD countries surveyed during the study, growth of the information sector could by no means be put down purely to developments in the services sector. The explanation is to be found in an increasing demand within the industrial sector for the activities of control, coordination and planning, or in other words for information activities.[19] Whatever the outcome of the debate on the information economy, the economics profession seems likely to make the decisive contribution, whether or not it has the last word.

References

1. Spence, A. Michael, An economist's view of information, in *Annual review of information science & technology*, ed. Carlos Cuadra, vol. 9, White Plains, New York, Knowledge Industry Publications, 1974, 57–78.
2. Samuelson, Paul, *Economics*, 11th edn, New York, McGraw Hill, 1980, 449.
3. Knight, Frank, *The economics of information and uncertainty*, New York, Harper Torchbooks, 1965.
4. Spence, op. cit., 58.
5. Harbury, Colin, *Economic behaviour: an introduction*, London, Allen & Unwin, 1980, 215.
6. Flowerdew, A. D. J. et al., *The pricing and provision of information*, London, British Library, 1984, 5. (R & D Report 20.)
7. Machlup, Fritz, Use, value and benefits of knowledge, in *Key papers in the economics of information*, ed. D. W. King et al., White Plains, New York, Knowledge Industry Publications, 1982, 245–65.
8. Spence, op. cit., 61–64.
9. Machlup, Fritz, *The Production and distribution of knowledge in the United States*, Princeton, New Jersey, Princeton University Press, 1962.
10. Porat, Marc Uri, *The Information economy: definitions and measurement*, Washington, DC, US Department of Commerce, Office of Telecommunications, 1978.
11. Organisation for Economic Cooperation and Development, *Trends in the information economy*, Paris, OECD, 1986, 16. (ICCP Report 11.)
12. Brinberg, H. R., Information in the United States: an industry serving industry, in *Information and the transformation of society*, ed. G. P. Sweeney, Amsterdam, North Holland, 1982, 265–86.
13. Gleave, David C. et al., *The impact of new technology on the labour market and demands for information services*, London, British Library, 1986.
14. Organisation for Economic Cooperation and Development, *Information activities, electronics and telecommunications technologies: impact on employment, growth and trade*, vol. 1, Paris, OECD, 1981.
15. Gleave et al., op. cit., 27.
16. Rubin, Michael Rogers, ed., *Information economics and policy in the United States*, Littleton, Colorado, Libraries Unlimited, 1984, 19.
17. Commission of the European Communities, *Europe faced with the challenge of the new information technologies: a community response*, Brussels, European Commission, 1979.
18. Strassmann, Paul A., *Information payoff: the transformation of work in the electronic age*, New York, Free Press, 1985, 9.
19. OECD, op. cit., 1986, 8.

CHAPTER 7

The information industry

The information industry is of growing significance to national and international economic activity. One of the hallmarks of advanced economies, it may be seen as a prerequisite to the development of information societies. This chapter will attempt to clarify the nature and status of the information industry, and to identify some of the major issues with which it is faced.

Why 'information industry'?

A major bone of contention in discussions on the information industry has to do with its relationship to services. As will be apparent from previous chapters, much depends upon interpretations of information, a treacherous and shifting concept. In what follows, therefore, no distinction will be drawn between information and data, with one person's information viewed as another person's data and vice versa. The essential distinction will lie in the field of services. It will be between physical-type services, such as hairdressing or car-valeting, and those which revolve around the commercial or value-added characteristics of information, for example business consultancies or information brokerages. The same approach will also be taken to the goods or products component of the information industry. The distinguishing features here will be use in support of information services or as products in their own right, and inputs of high-quality labour, advanced technology and research and development.

What is the information industry?

The information industry is essentially a product of the last quarter of the twentieth century. During the 1950s and 1960s, scientific and military research not only fuelled an ever-increasing demand for information but also led to breakthroughs in revolutionary new technologies. The use of these technologies spread far beyond their original scientific, technological, and military environments with, in the 1970s, a wide range of new application areas developing, notably in the financial services industry. By this time, the demand for information was exerting a kind of multiplier effect, with new applications and new business opportunities going hand in hand, and more and more companies entering the information industry.

Many of these organisations would have had only the most tenuous connections with information prior to this time, most likely through the generation and use of information for in-house purposes. Diversification of the market, and the tremendous increase in both the number and type of organisations involved, marked the appearance of an industry whose focus was not so much physical goods or services as information content or input. In the emergence of this industry, it was not the information factor *per se* but its application to innovatory or decision-making purposes that was important. While information in itself does possess economic characteristics, these become most apparent in applied situations, when information is combined with other resources, including other information. Thus, observed Brinberg, the product line of the information industry is information. It is an industry-serving industry.[1]

In early attempts at defining this industry, a clear distinction was drawn between the information industry and two related industries: the data processing industry and the knowledge industry.[1] Into the knowledge industry, for example, would have gone publishing, newspapers and broadcasting, all in fact plausible candidates for membership of the information industry. As for the information industry, this was divided into data processing services and data supply services. The former largely involved timesharing and related services, while the latter comprised such activities as data collection, analysis and research. Although these classifications are important, of more immediate interest is the implication that somehow the information industry, while engaged in the provision of services, had little to do with actual information content.[1] Questionable at the time, this distinctly restricted picture of the information industry would receive very short shrift today.

A more acceptable definition of the information industry was coined by the Information Industry Association (IIA) in the United States. This ascribed membership of the industry to those publishers and information service organisations offering information products and services by means of new technologies or innovative information-handling methods.[1] While having the advantage of including both products and services in its orbit, this is still overly restrictive in its stipulation of the use of new technologies. In this it is akin to those approaches which essentially have in mind an electronic information industry, such as was the subject of a recent report by the European Information Providers Association (EURIPA),[2] or which as a general rule would specify the presence of a nonprint medium or product.[3]

Easily the most comprehensive approach to definition is that of Zurkowski. Adapting earlier work by Day, he depicts the information industry in terms of eight segments: content services, content packages, facilitation services, information technologies, integrating technologies, communications technologies, communications channels, and broadcast channels.[4]

In displaying these eight segments as a map of the information industry, Zurkowski also distinguished between information content businesses, which accounted for three of the segments, and information technology businesses, which included the remaining five. The complete details can be found in the original work, but for present purposes an abbreviated version of Zurkowski's outline is reproduced as Tables 3 and 4 below. Although these do not capture the dynamic features of the original map, in which activities could overlap the boundaries of particular segments and shift from one segment to another, they should provide a reasonable indication of the nature and scope of the information industry. These are such as to embrace the creation and distribution of information goods and services, their support facilities and technologies, and a wide range of market and, on occasion, nonmarket transactions. Last, but by no means least, they should demonstrate that this is more than simply a service industry, being concerned both with the content of the information transmitted and with the processes and means of transmission.

Table 3. Information content businesses

Content services	News agencies; libraries; databases; information brokers.
Content packages	Books; newspapers; films; records; tapes; videodiscs.
Facilitation services	Data processing; timesharing; turnkey services.

Even this brief look at Zurkowski's classification gives a clear indication of the breadth of his vision of the information industry. His information content segments are not restricted by a requirement for any particular media format or any specified set of market conditions. Whereas he does distinguish between the two sets of industry segments, he nevertheless emphasises that the overall area is to be seen in its entirety as the information industry.

Table 4. Information technology businesses	
Information technologies	Computers, terminals, office equipment, printing and graphics.
Integrating technologies	Packet switching, modems, switchboards and digital switching.
Communications technologies	Radio, television, telephones and transmission systems.
Communications channels	Mail, telephone, telegraph and satellites.
Broadcast channels	Radio and television networks, multipoint distribution services.

It should be emphasised that these tables are abbreviated and indicative representations of Zurkowski's overall vision of the information industry. Understanding can be further enhanced with reference to the increasing significance of information markets and activities in the stimulation of economic growth and development. Hence, the European Community is embarked on pursuit of an information market policy for the EEC as a whole, a policy aimed at exploitation of the 'Information Services Sector'. This sector embraces a wide range of activities and participants, including libraries, publishers, computer service bureaux, database producers, distributors of information via the mass media, and the users of all these services.[5]

Two observations can be made about the contents of this sector. First, here is as good a general description of the information industry as any, and one which might serve as a working definition. Second, by introducing the concept of user involvement, the perspective on the information industry has been refined as well as widened. As a result, possible linkages to increasingly user-friendly and ever more intelligent technology are made more explicit. The same is true of the implications for such issues as the demise of the intermediary and the rise of the end user. In this total view, therefore, the information industry is a complex of goods and services – mainly, but not necessarily, profit-orientated – their associated technologies and structures, and the creators, producers, distributors and users thereof.

Components of the information industry

In 1981, the IIA in the United States identified six kinds of information company; these are reproduced in Table 5.

Table 5. Information companies by type[6]

1. Primary information companies

2. Secondary information companies

3. Computer-based information providers

4. Information retailers

5. Seminar/conference services

6. Information support services

Although, with the exception of support services, these are examples of pure information businesses rather than those providing the technology or technology-based facilitation services, they provide a useful starting point for a more detailed examination of the industry. Their functions can be briefly described as follows.

Primary information companies

These companies provide actual information, as opposed to bibliographical references. Their products or services come in such traditional forms as books and periodicals, and, in more modern vein, as online databases or databanks. Although these online systems possess the basic characteristic of shared access to information, by means of a terminal or modem on payment of the appropriate subscription and subsequent printing and connect charges, there are differences in the kinds of databases available. Those included within the orbit of primary information are known as source databases. Source databases contain direct information, either in full text, say as newspaper stories, as chemical formulae or as numeric values such as Stock Exchange information. They can also come in combined form as textual–numeric databases.[7]

Secondary information companies

As their name implies, these companies supply not the information itself but references or information on how to find it. This can be by means of a second type of online database, the so-called reference databases, which contain citations, abstracts and descriptions of projects or activities. Alternatively, it can involve the use of directories or yearbooks, that is the kind of reference tool found in that most fundamental of databases, a library.

Computer-based information companies

Companies of this type can provide access to a wide range of information, both primary and secondary. Typically, they include companies such as Bibliographic Retrieval Services (BRS), who buy limited rights in databases to be able to resell the information in specialist markets. The agreement between the distributor, that is the computer-based information company, and the primary or secondary publisher of the original information would lay down detailed operating conditions, including the cost of searches and the respective amounts paid to publisher and distributor. As a rule, the information would be mounted on a database accessible in the usual way by clients willing to pay for its enhancement in the form of indexes and more frequent updates.[8]

Information retailers

In many respects, this is the largest of the six categories of information company. As their name implies, information retailers sell information, and this can entail everything from providing factual information on demand to the design of complete library and information systems. The information factor aside, the unifying element in this category is consultancy, with information and advice being provided on a commercial basis to a wide range of customers. These consultancy activities tend to proliferate in the early stages of an industry's development. This is because, with the overheads involved, and the long-term nature of much of the investment, it can make sense to pay for the right kind of advice and thus avoid costly and possibly crippling mistakes.

Seminar/conference services

This self-explanatory class of activities is an important and growing component of the information industry. The fast-changing and often confusing environment of the information industry, and its associated technologies and services, means that there is a ready market for training activities of all kinds. The spread of potential suppliers includes academic institutions and professional associations as well as online information companies and private consultancy firms. In some cases, these are companies which began as users of the technology and then diversified into the training field.

Information support services

This is a very significant element of the information industry and one that is poised for considerable expansion in the immediate future. It includes the provision of timesharing and other computer processing facilities by computer bureaux, academic and public institutions, and large library cooperatives.

It has to be said, however, that while Table 5 is reasonably representative of those businesses that are more purely informational in nature, as a description of the information industry as a whole it leaves quite a lot to be desired. Notable absentees are the manufacturing components and those activities concerned with the delivery and transmission of information. To the purist, such activities play an enabling or supporting role in the information industry proper, and are best viewed as either information technologies separate from it or as service transactions based on these technologies. However, Zurkowski includes these technologies within his treatment of the information industry, and that is how they are regarded in this chapter. There is plenty of evidence that those engaged in these technological areas increasingly regard themselves as part of the information industry. The computer sector, for example, tends to see itself as part of an information industry whose products include hardware and software, storage devices and all manner of peripherals.

Also included in the information industry would be all those services made possible by developments in the new information and communications technologies – although in some cases comprising updated versions of older facilities – and ranging from teletext and videotex services to document delivery, electronic funds transfer and micropublishing. In fact, the increasingly coherent and interrelated nature of the industry can be discerned from developments within just one sector: the electronic information industry. Here, recent entrants have included publishing houses, research institutes, local and state governments, libraries, banks, professional associations and universities.[7]

Markets for the information industry

Another, and in some ways more fruitful, approach to the information industry is to view it from the standpoint of the markets in which it is trading. It is not all that easy to generalise about these markets, which like the goods and services involved are diverse phenomena. For purposes of illustration, however, two broad classes of market will be considered: markets for the technology and markets for the information itself.

Markets for information technology

In the case of information technology markets, the most obvious features are volatility and uncertainty. The pace of technical change, combined with the very high degree of competition, makes it extremely difficult to anticipate any but the most general of trends. On the basis of recent experience, however, certain observations can be made. A quite noticeable degree of change is already overtaking the basic structures and relationships within the computer industry. Where once hardware and software were accorded more or less equal status, the position so far as market prospects are concerned is one of the growing importance of software. In the United States, the software sector has exhibited growth rates of around 28 per cent a year, with the European experience being similar. Nor is this simply a matter of quantity, of the wholesale expansion of software *per se.* Indeed, such is the level of diversification within the software market that a recent projected study of software services had to be amended to one of software information retrieval services for publicly available databases, owing to the size of the software sector.[9]

Furthermore, where once the benefits of mass production led almost inevitably to the supply of large volume, standardised products and services, the picture today is much more fluid. Mass markets, of course, continue to be essential to the recovery of research and development costs, let alone production costs. However, in the United States the congruence of market conditions and technological developments has resulted in a trend towards the growth of customised products for specialist markets, and the subsequent growth of large numbers of small companies in order to meet the demand.[10] Similar trends are under way in Europe, and there should be a wide range of opportunities for the smaller company seeking to make its way in the information industry. Not that this by any means implies the imminent demise of the large multinational corporation. Quite apart from the mounting evidence of takeover bids and mergers in the information industry in the context of, say, hardware production, a company with an annual turnover of less than US$1 million is still regarded as being small.[10]

In practice, it will be those manufacturers who can respond to the increasingly sophisticated demands of users who will succeed most in these fast-changing markets for computer and related technologies. This will entail providing access to the latest networking technologies and user-friendly systems, across a range of specialist markets. Clearly, the requirement for

product and market differentiation will offer opportunities for thrusting new
entrepreneurs. However, the very need for such differentiation, along with the
requirement for leading-edge technologies, will put a high premium on
managerial inputs, particularly in the marketing sphere, with all the attendant
implications as regards the advantages of large-scale organisation.
Nevertheless, current developments in the microcomputer field, involving the
apparent demise of several household names and the emergence of new ones,
only serve to underline the fluidity and uncertainty of these markets.

Markets for information

So far as markets for information and data are concerned, a number of
relevant studies have been conducted in recent years. Of particular interest is
Anderla's work for the OECD, in the course of which he identified four key
markets for international data traffic: the elite market; the specialist market;
the business market; and the home market.[11] The details may be found in
Anderla's report, but the major findings were as follows.

The elite market. This market is exemplified by the activities of the big
information vendors, offering access to a wide range of online databases.
Anderla found that in 1983, despite the visibility of companies such as Dialog,
Systems Development Corporation (SDC), and BRS, growth rates had
declined and, indeed, saturation point may not be far off.[11] Therefore,
prospects in this elite market do not appear to be particularly promising.

The specialist market. This market is characterised by the provision of
up-to-date, accurate and highly specialised information to clients in such
fields as finance and the stock market, economics and credit rating. Its
attractions are encapsulated in its revenue figures, with the three largest
specialist providers, Reuters, Telerate and Quotron, generating revenues
some ten to twelve times those of the three largest 'information supermarkets',
Dialog, SDC and BRS. Less encouraging, however, are indications that this
market too is vulnerable to saturation, with supply already beginning to grow
faster than demand.[11]

The business market. So far as the business market is concerned, the situation
appears to be much more hopeful, with evidence of a considerable amount of
unsatisfied demand in the manufacturing, distribution, transport and small
business sectors. Currently, much of the demand for information within
organisations is being met by in-house provision at what is a relatively high
cost. Therefore, even allowing for growth in personal computing, Anderla
predicts a shift from less efficient in-house processing to the wholesale
farming out of information handling and computing of all kinds.[11] On this

basis, he concludes that the business market will be the most promising of all during the 1980s.

The home market. The home market is in many ways the most problematical of all the outlets for the information industry. It depends upon the successful introduction of videotex systems for use by domestic consumers, which in turn is dependent upon manifestation of the long-awaited surge of demand for the consumption of information at home. Experience to date has been disappointing, with, for example, British Telecom's Prestel system unable to attract many more than 20,000 subscribers.[11] The West German Bundespost's Bildschirmtext operation has drawn obvious lessons from the United Kingdom experience, aiming not simply to provide home access to information, but also linkages to electronic banking and shopping facilities.[11] Nevertheless, the results of market research conducted in the United States seem to indicate that an uphill struggle is ahead if American consumers are to be persuaded to pay for such a service. It may well be necessary for home information systems to be carried on the back of other, more commercially viable services, such as home banking. If this were possible, then the home market for information could really take off.

Market summary

In all these markets, competition is fierce and once a market has been lost it is unlikely to be recaptured.[12] The international market for computer hardware is dominated by the United States and Japan. As regards the direction of these trade flows, Western Europe is a heavy importer of such Japanese information products as microchips, computer hardware and consumer electronics. There is very little trade in the opposite direction, whether in technology or in information services. So far as trade between Europe and the United States is concerned, the picture varies from sector to sector. In the data processing field, the business is quite evenly distributed along national lines, with most countries seemingly able to hold their own in the domestic market. In the online information sector, on the other hand, the big three American companies, Lockheed Dialog, SDC, and BRS, dominate the world market.

The picture is different again in markets for highly specialised information. Hence, Reuters, a United Kingdom company, is the world leader in the field of financial information. Reuter's success lies in its ability to identify fast-moving markets and to supply them with up-to-the-minute information in such fields as currency movements, commodities, shipping, equity, bonds, gold, and oil. The company anticipated the advent of the end-user market by giving its customers access to the very latest technology. Banks, investment houses, finance companies and commodity dealers were given the choice of using their own hardware and accessing the Reuter's network by means of a special interface, or of using both hardware and software supplied by the company.[13]

The nature of the information industry ensures that Reuters does not have things all its own way, and it faces tough American competition from Telerate and IBM. Competition at home takes a different form, and one which illustrates another feature of these markets for information goods and services, namely segmentation. Thus, Citiservice, a similar if lower-level service, is available through Prestel, providing securities information and share prices for people whose need to know is not so urgent as to require the very latest and, therefore, expensive Reuters facilities.[14] This market segmentation demonstrates the potential profits to be made by combining technology and business acumen within the information industry. A further example, also in the United Kingdom, is the Software 800 telesoftware service, launched in 1983 by a consortium that included British Telecom and the East Midlands Allied Press. This service delivers software electronically to the home computer market over the Prestel network.[15]

Segmentation of this kind is likely to increase as the trend towards specialisation gathers momentum throughout the information industry. A further trend is likely to be towards the integration of information service provision, either through the development of integrated information suppliers (IISs) or with the advent of various types of information consortia. IISs are large database producers who decide to become independent of their existing network arrangements and set up as their own hosts. This is a risky operation and one which is open to only the largest of database producers, and then only under stringent market and technical conditions. Nonetheless, there is a definite trend in this direction and IISs now account for about half the total online industry.[16]

The emergence of information consortia began as a series of joint ventures involving partners in different countries, each offering different and complementary skills. Hence, Times Mirror Videotex Services in the United Kingdom and Informart in Canada have joined forces to market the Canadian company's videotex system, Telidon, in the United States.[17] Likewise, the American Telecommunications firm Telenet operates a worldwide medical information system with the Dutch database *Excerpta Medica*, supplies packet-switching equipment to the United Kingdom and Norwegian telecommunications companies, and is directly involved in the marketing of terminals manufactured in Belgium.[18] Impressive as they are in terms of marketing power and overall expertise, the real significance of such consortia could lie in their emergence as trading entities more powerful than any monopolies as yet seen.[19]

Finally, mention must be made of the increasing share of value-added activities within the information industry. Anderla has characterised this development in terms of a wholesale shift from mechanical to electronic technology, and a resulting diversification in both products and services.[20] With the automation of many traditional processes, timesharing bureaux have been able to attract business that was once the prerogative of book-keepers and accountants. In the process, they have added value to the service by the input of additional expertise or the use of more sophisticated software packages. Likewise, says Anderla, the most successful databases and operators are those that are able to provide value-added services in addition to basic information. These extra services would include forecasting tools, models and modelling aids, private data storage, reformatting facilities, training and professional advice.[20]

Characteristics of the information industry

Zurkowski has pointed out that, in addition to being media-independent, a repository of knowledge, orientated to the end-user, and heavily customised, the essence of an information company is that it perceives its basic product as information content.[21] This latter statement might seem to be something of a truism, as indeed do his further observations that information companies create their own products, and that these products are both decision-directed and priced on the basis of benefits provided.[21] However, these are all features which shed light on the particular nature and characteristics of the information industry. It creates its own products by means of the value-added processes carried out on the material. These products are decision-directed in that clients require information not for its own sake but because it helps in the fields of judgement and decision-making. Lastly, these prices are based more on what it would cost the user to reproduce the product than on any assessment of production costs.[21]

Finally, there is the fact that within its boundaries the information industry contains nonprofit as well as profit-making organisations. Listed among such organisations would be professional bodies and research associations, government departments and libraries, charities, and international organisations. Some of these bodies would see themselves as being part of the information industry and others would not, but whatever the case, they are not to be overlooked. In the United Kingdom alone, they account for nearly 30 per cent of firms in the electronic information industry.[21]

In his recent study of nonprofit organisations in the online database market, East calculated that some 50 per cent of databases in the United Kingdom were to be found in the nonprofit sector.[22] Even more significant is his suggestion that it is not so much profit or nonprofit orientation but market strategy that is the important factor in the development of such services.[22] In addition to a general inability to respond flexibly to market opportunities, most nonprofit databases suffer from those problems commonly associated with small firms, being product- rather than market-orientated, nondiversified, undercapitalised and noncompetitive.[22] This need not necessarily mean that all such organisations are doomed to bankruptcy, but it does link their fate to the actions of other agencies, such as database hosts, and indeed to the fate of those information intermediaries themselves under threat from end-user access.[22]

Problems facing the information industry

Although certain difficulties are 'sectorised', say in relation to the electronic information industry or to aspects of the international market, others may be regarded as problems for the industry as a whole. These can be listed as difficulties of operational environment, public–private interaction, technology, and the policy framework.

Operational environment

The problems of the operational environment are starkly highlighted by the fact that the European Community imports three times as much as it exports in this information area.[23] Indeed, the fact that this is such a one-sided process, with European firms unable to make much of an impact on the American and Japanese markets, may well be a disincentive to investment in the European information industry. Such disincentives can be readily appreciated given the size of the investment required for something like electronic publishing, which necessitates large-scale production for international markets.[23] There are additional disincentives in the current legal framework of the international information industry, where questions of ownership and security, legal liability, pricing and contracts, user protection and taxation all await some form of resolution. Although it would be unrealistic to expect any quick or easy solution to such problems, it should be possible for some generally agreed ground rules to be established. The European Community is giving the matter urgent attention through such means as its search for a Community information market policy.

Public–private interaction

Another problem for the information industry is the entry into the market of companies supported by public funds. The appearance of this subsidised competition can often seem like the final straw to firms already under pressure from both domestic and foreign rivals. It has led to a certain amount of polarisation on the merits of public versus private enterprise and, if anything, it can be expected to grow as an issue. A related matter, certain to exacerbate public–private tensions, is that of public procurement policies. Success in obtaining government purchasing contracts can be critical to the survival of many companies. Equally applicable to the concerns of database producers and hardware and software companies, procurement has an international dimension. It is considered essential to the success of current efforts to build up an effective European information industry capable of withstanding American and Japanese competition.

Although the current political climate would seem to favour profit organisations over nonprofit organisations, both in terms of revenue earned and employment created, there are other considerations. Not the least of these is the fact that, where database provision and information retailing are concerned, much of the value-added information which private firms find so profitable originates in the public sector and has been produced at public expense. Hence, it is argued, these public stores of information should be exploited in the common interest, with, say, national libraries and research institutes earning valuable foreign currency through repackaging and sale of the resources therein.

Technical difficulties

In this case, the term 'technical difficulties' is employed in a very wide sense, embracing economic and political factors as well as those of a more obviously technical nature. Two major sets of problems were identified in a EURIPA report published in 1985: those which appear to be in decline and those which are on the increase. Among the former were marketing weaknesses; hardware and software problems; lack of market information; lack of strategic coordination; and lack of market data and forecasts. Those problems seen to be worsening included the shortage and high cost of capital, systems incompatibility, shortage of skilled personnel, copyright, public procurement policies, and language barriers.[24] As several of these problems have already been encountered, attention will focus on those which have not.

The problem of marketing weakness covers everything from the insufficiently aggressive marketing behaviour of European information companies to fragmentation of the European market, not least owing to a lack of strategic coordination and policy at both national and European Community levels. It also involves cost factors related to the expense and inefficiency of producing information goods and services for small-scale national markets.

Hardware and software problems include difficulties over systems incompatibilities and the continued absence of a common command language for database access. Software is still on the whole insufficiently 'user-friendly' and, indeed, the EURIPA report drew a clear correlation between the continued existence of such inadequacies and the future business prospects of information brokerage companies.[24] The use and, more to the point, misuse of software, and of information in general, through such practices as 'downloading', form a large part of the copyright problem facing the information industry. Although analagous to earlier copyright difficulties over the re-use of printed materials bought by libraries, the problem is more severe in the case of electronic media. This is because of the ease with which the material may be duplicated. There is also the fact that while some sections of the industry, such as database hosts, seek to stamp out the practice, others, such as information retailers, depend on the information being available for resale, even if this leads to copyright problems. It is scarcely surprising that this was one of those problems that was found to be on the increase.

Nor will it come as any great surprise to be told that the information industry is facing shortages of key personnel, such as software engineers. This situation has come about directly as a result of the demand for more 'user-friendly' and 'intelligent' systems. The EURIPA report also noted the need for skilled 'go-betweens', for people who understood the technology and who could work and communicate effectively with both technical and nontechnical audiences.[25] The implications for the education and training sector seem to be encouraging.

Finally, there is the problem of language barriers, and the fact that English is the dominant language in use for both databases and software. While this has largely manifested itself as a problem for non-English speakers, the prospects for market expansion are increasingly dependent upon information being made available to users in their own languages. This is an area in which great hopes are pinned on the technology, particularly on developments in the field of artificial intelligence. Nevertheless, the problem is likely to worsen before such improvements are made.

The policy framework

The subject of information policy takes up the final chapter of the book, but a few words at this stage will not go amiss. Essentially, many of the problems encountered by the information industry stem from the absence of coherent national and international information policies. From a host of potential issues arising from this situation, two points seem to be worth making at this stage. First is the fact that, notwithstanding the high costs of collection, much publicly provided information is practically given away to anybody who wants it. Entire sectors of the information industry have developed on the basis of government information, obtained either free of charge or at nominal cost.

These information companies then add value to this information and resell it to a wide range of customers, included among whom can be those very government departments in which the information originated. Second is the fact that, while governments also have come to realise the revenue-earning potential of publicly funded information stores, there has been no great rush to devise the necessary policies to exploit these. In the United Kingdom, the ITAP report on *Making a business of information*[26] was a response to these opportunities, and it in turn has led to the formation of the Confederation of Information Communication Industries (CICI). Nevertheless, the whole question of information policy is something that has to be resolved on a much wider scale, involving economic and political action at a worldwide level.

Postscript

This chapter has sought to give a general overview of the information industry. In summing up, however, it is important to emphasise the continued strength of its more traditional elements. Thus, where total revenue from online databases in 1982 was of the order of US$11 billion, the worldwide market for printing and publishing was estimated to be well in excess of US$100 billion.[27] Looking in detail at these online figures, moreover, discloses that of the $11 billion taken in revenue, some 87 per cent was attributable to the sale of printed publications and offline products.[28] As for electronic publishing, despite undoubted growth potential, its revenues of £130 million per annum in the United Kingdom still amount to less than 3 per cent of those for conventional publishing.[29]

As for the future of the information industry, there seem to be reasonable grounds for optimism. It seems likely that it will remain a heterogeneous and diversified collection of markets, with expansion in the electronics sectors to be expected. It is difficult to foretell just when the expected breakthroughs in artificial intelligence and expert systems will occur. When this happens, however, the outcome need not necessarily be a reduction in the scale of the industry, through the demise of its intermediary element. It is just as likely that new and qualitatively different roles will arise, for instance in decision-support and problem-solving activities. What seems certain, however, is that whatever its shape, and whoever is involved, the information industry is here to stay.

References

1. Brinberg, H.R., Information in the U.S.: an industry serving industry, in *Information and the transformation of society*, ed. G. P. Sweeney, Amsterdam, North Holland, 1982, 265–86.

2. Business International, *Survey of the European information industry: its electronic developments*, Geneva, Business International, 1984.

3. Strauch, Helena M., Entrepreneurship in the information industry, in *Careers in information*, ed. Jane Spivack et al., White Plains, New York, Knowledge Industry Publications, 1982, 73–101.

4. Zurkowski, Paul G., Integrating America's infostructure, *Journal of the American Society for Information Science*, 35, 3, 1984, 170–78.

5. Commission of the European Communities, *Discussion paper on a Community information market policy*, Brussels, European Commission, 1985.

6. Strauch, op. cit., 78.

7. Business International, op. cit., 16.

8. Strauch, op. cit., 80.

9. Business International, op. cit., 158.

10. McClellan, Stephen T., Sea change in the information industry, *Datamation*, International Edition, June 1982, 88–99.

11. Anderla, G., 'The international data market revisited', Paper presented to a special session of the Committee for Information, Computer and Communications Policy, OECD, 1983, unpublished.

12. McClellan, op. cit., 88.

13. Business International, op. cit., 32–33.

14. Ibid., 34.

15. Ibid., 74.

16. Ibid., 4.

17. Anderla, op. cit., 27.

18. Ibid., 26.

19. Ibid., 28.

20. Ibid., 16.

21. Zurkowski, op. cit., 171–72.

22. East, Harry, Nonprofit organisations in the U.K. online database market, *Aslib Proceedings*, 38, 9, September 1986, 327–34.

23. Commission of the European Communities, op. cit., 1.

24. Business International, op. cit., 97.

25. Ibid., 83.

26. Information Technology Advisory Panel, *Making a business of information*, London, HMSO, 1984.

27. Anderla, op. cit., 6.

28. British Library, *The British Library strategic plan*, London, British Library, 1986, 10.

29. Anderla, op. cit., 10.

CHAPTER 8

Information management

Information management has become what in modern parlance would be known as a 'buzzword', an inevitable consequence of which has been some confusion as to its meaning and application. Its current prominence dates back to 1977, when the US Commission on Federal Paperwork found that many of the problems facing the Federal bureaucracy were in fact attributable to poor information management.[1] Efforts to deal with this problem included enactment of the Paperwork Reduction Act, 1979, and the establishment of positions for information managers within the Federal service. Important as such developments were, however, they would not have been sufficient in themselves to address the challenge posed by the need to manage information and its related resources.

At one level, this was a more complex version of a challenge long familiar to the library and information professions. As such it was essentially a threefold problem: information diffusivity, where systems and users were tending to become problem-orientated rather than discipline-orientated; the heterogeneity of information carriers; and the exploitation of information through tertiary processing. At another level, the increasing complexity of these problems was in itself merely the outcome of changes within society as a whole – changes arising from the institutionalisation of information, and from its recognition as a source of competitive advantage and of profit. Added to this was the impact of the new information technologies, at once a means of controlling the ceaseless output of information, and of adding to the flood. Therefore, the problems posed by the need to manage the information resource, while initially a matter for individual organisations, would have considerable implications for society as a whole.

What is information management?

The concept of information management is one of realising the benefits of a valuable resource by subjecting it to the standard managerial processes and controls. To be effective, moreover, this must go beyond such procedural matters as collection, storage and dissemination to address the substantive issues of information use and its contribution to the attainment of organisational aims and objectives.[1] As such, therefore, information management is to be distinguished from management information systems (MIS). MIS is a means of providing particular types of information to clearly defined levels of management. Hence it is both narrower in scope and more restrictive in concept than information management, whose context is that of the entire organisation. However, because they are in all essentials the same thing, no distinction will be drawn between 'information management' and 'information resource management'. Whereas the shorter of the two terms will be preferred, the working definition employed will be a variant of one originally coined in respect of information resource management. Accordingly, information management is defined as the planning, budgeting, organising, directing, training, and control associated with information. The term encompasses both information itself and related resources such as personnel, equipment, funds and technology.[2]

A noticeable feature of this definition, and of the more useful alternatives, is their essential duality. Hence, Broadbent defined information management as both management of the information process and of data resources.[3] Lytle later described this in terms of information assets, that is the content of information, and information resources, the equipment, supplies and people through which an organisation handles its information.[4] To Marchand, the dichotomy lay between process and product, between human aspects and those focussing on systems. It is in their coordination for the improvement of organisational decision making that the vital contribution of information management is to be found.[5]

Why 'information management'?

Another, and perhaps even more noticeable, feature of these descriptions of information management is that they could be employed with equal facility in respect of management itself. If this is so, then why all the fuss about information management? Again, whereas few would dispute that information is an element critical to the decision-making process, surely this has always been the case, so why invent a new term to describe its exploitation and control? There are two basic answers to these questions. In the first place, there is indeed little point in distinguishing between the two terms, because information management is just what its name implies: it is a form of management. Thus Marchand refers to the coordinated management of processes and products,[5] while Horton talks of the emergence of a new management function, with its place on the organisation chart and its designated authorities and responsibilities.[6] In the second place, however, information management is a special form of management, and one which owes its importance to the social and environmental changes that form the subject of this book. As Melody has observed, entire industries and major sectors of the economy are now devoted to information, while decision-making at all levels – governmental, corporate and individual – is increasingly dependent on highly complex information and communication systems.[7] Consequently, it was inevitable that there should be some kind of realignment of factors in the overall resource matrix, with information emerging as the critical one. Hence, 'information management'.

The elements of information management

In attempting to introduce information management into any organisation, much depends on the ability of its 'culture' and structure to accommodate changes in function and in organisational aims and objectives. This is unlikely to happen without the identification of those areas of operation truly critical to information management. From a confusing spread of potential candidates can be isolated such key areas as data processing, word processing, telecommunications, paperwork and records management, libraries and information centres, office systems, external information services, and control of all information-related expenditures. It is the planning and coordination of all these diverse elements, of the technologies, the human expertise, and the resources and systems for their use, that go to make up the phenomenon of information management.

The principles of information management

In isolating both the general thrust of information management and its component elements, it is possible also to detect certain principles upon which it is founded. Central to these is the notion of information as resource and, indeed, as a resource whose utilisation is critical to the exploitation of all other resources. Another basic principle concerns the primacy of this information resource, and the need to distinguish ends from means, the information itself from the means by which it is delivered. A third principle relates to the pervasive characteristics of information, a corollary of which is the integrated management of all resources. A further, and related, principle is that of accountability and the fixing of responsibility for each and every aspect of information management upon carefully specified individuals.

Perceptions of information management

In spite of the current level of interest in information management, it is still virtually impossible to gauge with any accuracy the extent to which the strategic nature of the information resource is generally appreciated. The development of a voluminous and expanding literature on the subject suggests that, behind all the hyperbole, a genuine trend is developing. However, it is impossible to tell whether this denotes a growth of interest in information management or simply an increased awareness of information. It could be argued, of course, that the one follows naturally from the other, in that information awareness, no matter how rudimentary, leads inevitably to its perception, first in resource, and then in management, terms.

Nor is the evidence for such a progression any longer confined to developments taking place within the United States. Job classifications, organisational structures, educational and training initiatives, and the increasingly international character of the literature all testify to a general upsurge of interest in information and its management. In a good many cases this has led to a search for technological solutions, with unrealistic expectations engendered by the inappropriate application of hardware to complex organisational and managerial problems. Frequently, this has succeeded only in creating new and even more perplexing problems, while leaving the original difficulties untouched. The continued recurrence of such activity serves to emphasise the limited levels of understanding of the nature of information-driven change, whether at the organisational level or within society as a whole.

So far as the management of information within organisations is concerned, the picture is clouded both by the circumstances of individual organisations and by their varied perceptions of what it is that constitutes information management. Nor is this situation greatly helped by the existence of a wide range of professional perceptions of the term. This is understandable in view of the many attractions and, indeed, the interdisciplinary character of information management, but it adds further confusion to an already complex area. Thus, even in the case of those professions whose information management credentials, if not exactly impeccable, are more plausible than most, there can be considerable variation in the range and type of work that is carried out. Librarianship and information science are obvious examples, but the same is true of management services and computer professionals, by no means all of whom possess the integrative skills required to manage the use, as well as the processing, of information. In the race by various professional groups to 'colonise' the information management area, early success has gone to those with a quantitative and technological approach, rather than to groups whose interest lies primarily in the resource and service aspects of information. Should this trend continue unchecked it would have serious implications for the future development of information management.

Constraints on development

Although people will claim that information management has been around for centuries, as viewed in this chapter it is a combination of human, organisational and technological factors which only became a practical possibility during the 1980s. As such it might seem a little premature to be talking about constraints on development, particularly when seen from the perspectives of data processing or management services organisations, where the pace of change has at times been phenomenal. Be that as it may, the key to information management resides in its recognition of the resource characteristics of information, and it is upon progress in the exploitation and application of this information resource that success should be judged. Therefore, if the advance towards this goal has been in any way retarded it is reasonable to speculate on the nature and existence of potential constraints.

In fact, Marchand has identified seven such constraints applicable in the context of public organisations.[5] These can be characterised as theoretical, methodological, organisational, human, legal, fiscal, and political. This list appears to be equally relevant to the circumstances of organisations operating outside the public service environment. As is the case with the principles of information management, there is a certain amount of overlap between these categories. This is particularly evident as concerns the human and political constraints, which are both largely concerned with people, and with their likely reactions to the kinds of change which would follow the introduction of information management. Organisational, legal and fiscal constraints, on the other hand, derive from within these respective structures and from their flexibility in the face of proposed new policies and practices. As Marchand makes clear, however, the removal of all such constraints can be achieved only on the basis of a clear and realistic perception of the problems and issues involved. Quite clearly, the absence of such a perception would in itself constitute a constraint of fundamental and even crippling proportions.

Implementation

Horton and Marchand have provided a wealth of instruction on the practical side of information management. As regards methodology, Horton has identified the five major steps in information management as: inventory all information assets and resources; cost all existing information technologies and supporting resources; establish the value of each major information asset *vis-à-vis* high priority corporate needs; establish overlaps and gaps in information flows; and target existing systems, records and files for integration in support of decision-making and problem-solving.[6] In empirical studies of the application of such methods, Marchand has detected the same three-phased approach as operating within both public and private organisations, namely the integration of responsibilities for the management of information technology, an emphasis on user support tools and needs, and an emphasis on information use and content.[8]

Phase one really marks acceptance of the need for information management, and for the realignment of administrative structures in order to integrate the management of data, paperwork, office automation and telecommunications under a single function controlled by a designated, high-level manager. Phase two has been greatly accelerated by the availability of desktop technology, especially with the development of microcomputers and associated high-level software, thus enabling end-users to become their own information processors. The third phase involves maturation of the information management process, with the emergence of sophisticated decision-support systems, which, employing the latest advances in artificial intelligence, are already being hailed as knowledge-management systems.

It should be emphasised that, while clearly significant in an operational context, these phases are employed here mainly to indicate the scope of the implementation process. Implicit in this approach is the need to know what makes a particular organisation 'tick', and the ways in which specific shifts in emphasis, whether in policy, structures or methods, will affect progress towards organisational goals. If not quite a matter of trial and error, there is a distinct incremental dimension to information management. That it should be implemented incrementally or not at all would appear to conform both with the dictates of commonsense and with current practice.

Planning, budgeting and accounting

An overview chapter such as this can do little more than sketch the broad outlines of information management, while perhaps attempting to highlight some of its principal functional areas. In view of its fundamental resource characteristics, three such areas critical to the operation of information management are planning, budgeting and accounting. Each of these three areas will now be briefly considered.

Planning for information management

The case for information management is grounded in the concept of information as resource, with consequent cost implications. Better information management can frequently mean less information, an underlying objective being a reduction of the costs involved in its collection, storage and dissemination. An essential prerequisite to the improved management of information, therefore, is a planning process which takes into account not only the goals, methods and expected outcomes of the exercise, but also organisational aims and objectives, information resources, needs and use, and any constraints which might be operable. To be fully effective, moreover, such planning should operate on a clear understanding of the cost and value aspects of information and on a full appreciation of the qualities inherent in the data resource.

Horton lists certain attributes of data germane to the planning process and, specifically, to the trade-offs inevitable in the determination of information requirements – compromises involving factors such as level of detail, cost, quality and precision.[6] As with all planning, the general objective is to close the gap between expectations of the benefits accruing from the process and the utility of what is actually provided. It is essential also that such planning and the policies which result from it are related closely to both the 'culture' and the business plan of the organisation concerned. These information policies should be organisation-wide in scope and should relate to all aspects of data (collection, creation and security); information processing equipment; information systems and services; and the roles and responsibilities of management, users and staff in the management of information assets and resources.

Budgeting for information management

If the full potential of the information resource is to be realised, it must be integrated into the budgetary process. This, however, is by no means as straightforward as it sounds, not least because information costs are frequently subsumed within other costs. Nevertheless, use of the proper techniques can help to extract information costs and produce an information line item for the organisational budget. It can also enhance overall budgetary performance and, by implication, the management of the entire resource base of the organisation. In essence, therefore, budgeting for information costs involves identification of those activities which are data-handling in character, and costing them on the principle that, in addition to salary, everything an employee requires to do the job of creating and processing data and information should be counted as a cost.[9]

The basic objective of such activities is to keep track of organisational expenditures to enable management to know exactly how much money is being spent by each particular department or individual and for what purpose. The need to control expenditure has resulted in the formulation of strategies such as zero-based and incremental budgeting. Zero-based budgeting operates on the principle that no programme or activity is immune from regular scrutiny and review, with the possibility of curtailment or closure applying to all. Incremental budgeting assumes that the budget for any one year is based on that for the previous year plus some increment to be negotiated. As Horton points out, information budgeting is subject to a number of influences, not least differences in administrative style. In any event, two major approaches can be identified: input-orientated and output-orientated information budgeting.

Input-orientated, or 'bottom-up', approaches tend to focus upon the control of familiar, clearly-defined categories of resource, such as personnel, equipment or supplies, and are not concerned with output, that is with the uses to which these are put. Apart from the fact that these categories, or objects of expenditure, can be of limited value in highlighting information expenditures, the input approach says little about the relationship between such expenditures and information value. Output-orientated, or 'top-down', approaches, on the other hand, put considerable emphasis on planning and performance-evaluation, on the less tangible, more qualitative aspects, such as the perceived value of information to analytical and decision-making activities.[9] Viewed from the standpoint of information management, the output-orientated approach has much to commend it. However, while requiring imagination, both approaches can be applied in a step-by-step fashion, which, while thorough, makes no great demands for overnight changes to organisational structure.

Accounting for information management

It is also the case that, while it is essential to effective information management, introduction of a cost accounting structure need not entail any drastic departure from existing methods. Essentially there are two aspects to information accounting: a cost structure, such as will reveal the significant expenses of the organisation and thus facilitate the pursuit of value for money; and performance measures and techniques for assessing the process.

In the determination of information costs, both 'bottom-up' and 'top-down' approaches are employed. The 'bottom-up' method uses the 'object of expenditure' system to record the nature of any financial transaction, irrespective of the purpose for which the money is spent. This has the effect of bringing the possible variety of costs involved in any transaction under one established head, which in all likelihood will not facilitate detailed accounting controls; for example, purchase of a motor car being placed under 'equipment', ignoring such additional expenses as road tax or delivery charges. The 'top-down' approach, on the other hand, starts by asking a series of questions about the organisation, the particular object under consideration, and the role, nature and format of the information resources required. Only after these questions have been answered is recourse made to the object of expenditure levels for purposes of costing.

As regards the establishment of standardised information costs, and the techniques needed to measure the variance of actual costs from planned costs, there is still much work to be done. Hence, whereas in the United States a distinction between 'core' and 'noncore' costs is seen as essential, perceptions of what constitutes what are highly subjective and can vary from one agency to another.[9] Moreover, the American experience has been that, notwithstanding the attractions of output-orientated approaches in terms of information management, both input and output methods are needed. This is because, for all their failings, the conventional object of expenditure categories on the output side can lend themselves to costing for information purposes, while alternative output approaches, such as use typologies, are susceptible to individual judgement. As Horton explains, we lack essential meta-information, or information on information, such as data descriptions, categories and entities, which would enable us to fully understand the information resource. We also need clarification of the information element of those costs frequently concealed within such budget categories as 'other services'.[9]

Therefore, accounting and budgeting for the information resource are integral components of information management. Indeed, it is only when the planning and utilisation of information can operate on the basis of adequate cost control and reporting that organisations can aspire realistically to information management.

Postscript

This brief overview of information management has sought to portray the subject in its proper interdisciplinary context, rather than view it as a kind of updated librarianship. As with the technology which it uses to such good effect, information management is a mixture of the old and the new, and its essential novelty arises in the enabling characteristics of a different mix of factors, and a set of relationships in which the information factor is seen to hold the key to organisational change and performance. Information management is concerned with using information in support of the aims and objectives of individual organisations. Entailing the management of information assets as well as information resources, it is concerned with the planning and administration of all kinds of data, as well as with information systems and services. It also involves the management of converging technologies and, indeed, of the impact of changes brought about within the organisation as a result of the implementation of information management. Information management is, therefore, a strategic activity, the true significance of which is reflected in its growing prominence within the organisational hierarchy of a wide range of organisations.

While a special and highly significant aspect of management, however, information management is no more a panacea for existing management ills than are the new information technologies. Nor, indeed, has the development of information management by any means run its course. Already there is talk not just of information management but also of knowledge management, based on perceptions of an allegedly higher-order relationship between information and knowledge and advances in intelligent systems and knowledge engineering. The really radical element in all this may well be not a further development in management theory and practice but changes of the nature anticipated by Daniel Bell nearly two decades ago, and the emergence of a society whose central axis is codified knowledge. Viewed in such a context, information management could well acquire both new meaning and new significance.

References

1. Commission on Federal Paperwork, The paperwork problem, in *Information management in public administration*, ed. Forest W. Horton, Jr and Donald A. Marchand, Arlington, Virginia, Information Resources Press, 1982, 28–44.
2. Lytle, Richard H., Information Resource Management: 1981–1986, in *Annual review of information science & technology*, vol. 21, ed. M.E. Williams, White Plains, New York, Knowledge Industry Publications, 1986, 309–36.
3. Broadbent, Marianne, Information management and educational pluralism, *Education for Information*, 2, 1984, 209–27.
4. Lytle, op. cit., 310.
5. Marchand, in Horton and Marchand, op. cit., 58–69.
6. Horton, in Horton and Marchand, op. cit., 45–57.
7. Melody, William H., The context of change in the information profession, *Aslib Proceedings*, 38, 8, August 1986, 223–30.
8. Marchand, Donald A., *A manager's guide for implementing information resource management (IRM) in a state agency*, Columbia, South Carolina, College of Business Administration, University of South Carolina, 1984, 51–57.
9. Horton, Forest W., Jr, *Information resources management: concept and cases*, Cleveland, Ohio, Association for Systems Management, 1979, 132–38.

CHAPTER 9

Information in the international environment

This chapter seeks to provide an international dimension to some of the information issues raised in previous chapters. It is also concerned with wider aspects of international relations, linked increasingly to the social, economic, political and cultural ramifications of the information factor. After a brief look at some general assumptions, the chapter turns to its two main themes: information developments and their implications for the developed world, and relations between the industrialised nations and the emerging countries of the Third World.

Some general assumptions

This entire volume has been anchored in certain assumptions as to the importance of information and its associated technologies to the development and prosperity of nations. These assumptions are held to be as valid for developing as for developed countries. Hence, Narasimhan has emphasised the importance for developing nations of an understanding of the socioeconomic significance of the technologies that underlie both the industrial culture of the West and, more recently, information technology.[1] In the West, meanwhile, advances within these new technologies have become the pacemaker for change in modern economies. This is easily illustrated by the phenomenon of digitisation, which is transforming policies and practices in all sectors.

However, the pervasive significance of these information factors is seen to best effect in the worldwide prominence of informatics. The growing importance of this subject is reflected in the establishment of a United Nations agency with responsibility for informatics matters. This body, the Intergovernmental Bureau of Informatics (IBI), defines informatics as:

> the rational and systematic application of information to economic, social and political development.[2]

105

While it is the case that membership of the IBI is overwhelmingly comprised of developing nations, its activities are of much wider significance. Indeed, the sheer importance of informatics ensures that it has gained attention in government and international circles as a whole, as the world attempts to get to grips with the problems it has raised.

These problems are viewed here in the context of a global information environment. Whereas it would seem to be in everybody's interest for international information flows to function efficiently and equitably, there is wide variation in the response of individual governments and groups of governments. These differences are too complicated for any simple classification in terms of the conflicting interests of, say, the developed and the developing nations. On some occasions, they may be explained along straightforward economic or political lines, involving disputes between nations at similar or, indeed, widely different levels of development. On others, the very perception of what legitimately constitutes national interest could itself be at issue, with some nations emphasising cultural or philosophical aspects at the expense of more material considerations. On one thing there does seem to be agreement, however, and that is the importance of the information transfer process to all concerned.

The developed world

As used here, the term 'developed world', or alternatively the 'North', consists of North America, Europe, the USSR, Japan, Australia, and New Zealand. In it live one-quarter of the world's population, with 90 per cent of its manufacturing capacity and four-fifths of its income.[3] In this 'First World' of developed, mainly free-market economies, the importance of information and trade in information goods and services is now largely beyond dispute. Its vital contribution to economic growth and welfare has resulted in the development of national, and on occasions international, informatics plans. It has also led to the growth of protectionism and restraint of trade, as governments strive to defend or develop national stakes in a burgeoning market. The focus of these developments has been sharpened by two considerations. The first is the genuinely international character of the information trade, and the second the revolutionary and thus inherently disruptive impact of the technologies involved. Hence, where change and instability in markets, technologies, business practices and legal frameworks have interacted with national interests, the outcome has all too often been one of both commercial and political mayhem.

Indeed, fears have been expressed lest the current climate of animosity and mistrust lead to the outbreak of an information war before the end of the 1980s. In the event, the dispute would involve serious conflict between the developed nations, some of them fellow members of the OECD, one of the functions of which is to prevent such misunderstandings from arising. Lest such talk be seen as alarmist, let us consider three pieces of supporting evidence: the emergence of national informatics plans, the erection of barriers to trade, and the actual experience of those finding themselves at the receiving end of such measures.

National informatics plans

Considerable emphasis was given to the development of informatics by publication of the now famous report written in 1978 by Nora and Minc.[4] The major thrust of this report was twofold. The authors emphasised the critical importance of the new information technologies for economic and social development, calling for nothing less than the 'informatisation' of French society. Second, and no less important, was their concern with the extent to which key areas of the French microelectronics industry were vulnerable to foreign control, notably through the market power of American multinationals such as IBM. Accordingly, the report contained a series of recommendations aimed at protecting the national interest and ensuring a genuine French presence in the field of high technology. Recommendations of this type subsequently found their way into the policy statements of other European countries, for example the Alvey Programme for Advanced Information Technology in the United Kingdom.

What was so noticeable about the French proposals, however, was their avowedly mercantilist character, aiming not simply at the general protection of trade, but at direct confrontation with those externally controlled multinational companies that were perceived as the most immediate threat to national interests. Not that there is anything inherently wrong with such policies, nor indeed with any reasonable action taken to preserve economic independence and protect employment in what, by common consent, are key sectors. The difficulty is, however, that once taken, such actions tend to result in counteractions and reprisals, with subsequent damage to the market as a whole. All trading relationships exist on the basis of mutual advantage and interdependence. In the case of information markets, however, where more than simply economic considerations are involved, the result can be seen not just as restraint of trade but as an abrogation of the natural human rights of access and expression.

In directly challenging the activities of the multinational companies, therefore, the French were among the first to raise what subsequently was to become an issue of worldwide concern, that of national sovereignty. Thus, without a national information and communications industry, countries would become dependent upon outside forces, whether for the provision of hardware and software products, the supply of data processing and information services, or the protection and security of data. Within a year of publication of the Nora–Minc report, the Canadians emerged with an equally radical defence of national sovereignty. The Clyne Report pointed out the dangers of economic and political dependency, balance of payments problems, data security, and unemployment as inevitable consequences of relying on the information and data processing facilities of other nations.[5] In the Canadian case, moreover, there was the abiding fear of becoming a 'branch plant' economy, an economic satellite of the United States. This situation was given particular emphasis, with the revelation that something like 90 per cent of all data generated in Canada was being processed on computers located south of the border in the United States. The opportunity cost in employment terms alone was a powerful argument for some kind of national response, with estimates running into many thousands of jobs lost to the United States information industry.[5]

Employment was also a major consideration in the European Community's response to the problems and opportunities inherent in the international market for information goods and services. Quite apart from the interests of individual member states, the economics of the information trade frequently demand large-scale production within homogeneous markets, indeed just those conditions which the European Community was intended to foster. In reality, however, the Community is a loose alliance of twelve individual member states, with differences in language, levels of development and national interests. Faced with the challenge of American and Japanese information industries, tempered in the heat of large and fiercely competitive internal markets, no single European country could aspire to having much of an impact in the international information arena. Indeed, as the 1970s drew to a close, prospects for a European-based information industry were at best mixed, owing largely to fragmentation of the market and continuing national rivalries. Realisation of the serious nature of the challenge facing the region as a whole led the European Commission to embark on its own supranational informatics plan.

The basis for action lay in a report prepared by the Commission in November 1979 entitled *European society faced with the challenge of the new information technologies.*[6] Known colloquially as the Dublin Report, this proposed an overall target of one-third of the world information market by 1990, and among its more specific recommendations were standardisation of components used in computing, removal of nontariff barriers between member countries of the EEC, open competition for government contracts, more money for research and development, and the establishment of an ISDN.[6] Accepted in 1980 by the Council of Ministers, this programme can be seen to have three broad aims: the initiation of measures to prepare society as a whole for changes which are inevitable; establishment of a single, uniform market within the community; and creation of new markets and new industrial capacity.[7]

A considerable effort has been made to implement these proposals, as evidenced for example by wholesale public education programmes with regard to the new technologies, by legislation designed to facilitate the mobility of labour, and by attempts to harmonise the different technical standards obtaining within the various telecommunications jurisdictions. Among the more notable successes have been the Research into Advanced Communications in Europe (RACE) programme and the European Research Programme for Information Technology (ESPRIT). RACE made considerable progress towards objectives targeted for completion by the end of 1985. These included the implementation of common telecommunications standards; the opening up of public procurement contracts to competition; and establishment of advanced data transmission systems between national and Community organisations.[8] ESPRIT was launched in 1984 with the aim of promoting collaboration between European researchers in the field. This collaboration was to occur at the precompetitive stage, that is before individual organisations in the various countries were required to compete for markets or for development funding. Again, five specific areas of activity were targeted: advanced microelectronics, software, advanced information processing, office systems, and computer-integrated manufacture.[8]

In view of the nature of the European Community, these proposals have required not just coordination but also a fair amount of pump-priming in areas where national governments or individual companies have either been unable or reluctant to act. These measures have lent more than a hint of credibility to such notions as information-based economies and societies. Despite these efforts, however, it could well be a case of too little too late, with, for example, the technology correspondent of the *Guardian* newspaper predicting that in the information industry of ten years' time, Europe could well be nowhere.[9] There are other opinions, of course, and even if Large is right, then surely this is all the more reason for action at the Community level? To be effective, however, such action must be designed to facilitate trade and technological developments, rather than obstruct them, otherwise they will be self-defeating. Unfortunately, in a world where nations are increasingly interdependent, and in markets which depend upon openness and the free exchange of goods and information, the trend towards the erection of barriers to trade seems to be everywhere on the increase.

The erection of trade barriers

In view of the central importance of telecommunications to the information industry, recent technological and commercial developments in that field offer a useful basis for understanding the rationale behind such protectionist behaviour. In the past, the dominant force in the discussion of telecommunications issues has been technological, with the major focus being on the supply side, and on such questions as access to international markets. However, the pace of technological development has shifted the focus of attention towards the demand side of the equation, and to the needs and interests of telecommunications users. Particularly significant has been the onset of digitisation and of 'dematerialisation', that is the growing importance of software over hardware in telecommunications equipment.[10] A second and related development is the importance of trade in both information goods and services. Although trade in information services has not yet been brought within the provisions of the General Agreement on Tariffs and Trade (GATT), there is strong pressure from the United States and others for this to happen. Their inclusion would seem to be only a matter of time. Action is also needed on the goods side, however, where the right not just to sell equipment in particular markets, but also to connect equipment to national and international networks, carries considerable implications for information policy.

Trade in information goods and services is subject to a wide range of restrictions, with both tariff and nontariff barriers in operation. Among the more obvious areas of restriction are telecommunications tariffs, excessive regulation and unfair competition, discriminatory technical standards, and privacy and data protection legislation. Also included would be attempts to restrict the flow of data and information across national borders, and controls imposed in the interests of cultural integrity and national sovereignty.

Telecommunications tariffs. The major area of difficulty with tele-communications tariffs concerns charges levied for the use of private leased circuits. These are communications or data processing networks leased from common carriers and reserved for the exclusive use of the customer concerned. The major users of such circuits have been the large multinational companies that depend upon access to the latest telecommunications technology in order to transmit information and data efficiently all over the world on an around-the-clock basis. In the past, these circuits have been available at flat monthly rates, which for large volume users have proved an attractive alternative to international telex charges, which are based on connect time. However, with the growth of international trade in services, and with it the profits of multinational companies, national telecommunications administrations, or PTTs, have grown increasingly unhappy with this arrangement. As a result, the availability of private leased circuits can no longer be taken for granted, nor indeed can the conditions under which they will be made available in the future.

In the matter of tariffs, however, it is hard to understand why, for example, the same telecommunications facilities can vary so markedly in price on either side of the Atlantic. It can cost up to ten times as much to hire a private circuit in Europe as it can in the United States. In some Middle Eastern countries the cost can run at as much as 15 times the American level.[11] Again, while the PTTs are understandably anxious to increase their own share of the profits from this highly lucrative sector, their charges would seem to be rather less related to the cost of providing the service than to estimates of what the market will bear. Current attempts to replace circuit rental arrangements with a system of volume-sensitive pricing are greeted with growing irritation on the part of the user community. In effect, this would mean that the tariffs levied would be based upon either the volume of traffic passing over the line or the speed of operation of the transmission equipment in use. To the users, such changes of pricing policy appear both illogical and discriminatory, and some argue that data transmission costs could rise by as much as 700 per cent, thereby rendering the entire process uneconomic.[12] Furthermore, the fact that this shifting complex of pricing policies contains cross-subsidies designed to prop up otherwise nonviable local telecommunications services in the countries concerned does little for user morale.[13]

Excessive regulation and unfair competition. Such restrictive practices run contrary not just to changing technological and regulatory trends but also to the interests of users. The term 'user' is a somewhat ambiguous one, but here it refers to those organisations that are paying for the privilege of using private leased lines. Although, owing to differences in configuration, levels of sophistication and operational procedures, no two such networks are the same, in certain respects their needs are identical. Hence, all users depend upon cooperation from those PTTs within whose jurisdictions their operations are conducted, and all require as much flexibility as possible in the operating conditions laid down for the purpose. A fundamental problem is the considerable variation in operating conditions and, specifically, in respect of two questions: what equipment can be connected at what points in the network; and to what extent can spare capacity be resold to other potential users or put to different use within the information industry?

From the viewpoint of the PTTs, many of whom have invested considerable sums of public money in the development of their own public data networks, the picture can be very different. Not only is there the need to recoup some of these costs, but also there are excellent business opportunities to be exploited. After all, the multinational companies are in the information business to make a profit, so why should the PTTs not attempt to do the same? In reply, the users would argue that while there is nothing wrong with the pursuit of profit, the imposition of restrictions on the information market is inherently bad for business, with, in the long run, the PTTs, the user community and the public being the losers. Burgess, of the Bank of America, one of the leading advocates of user autonomy, argues for freedom of interconnection between public and private networks, the shared use of private leased circuits, and the limiting of equipment homologation, that is operating standards, to matters of safety. Last but not least, he has called for the entire matter to be taken out of the hands of the PTTs.[13]

Another reason why international information companies remain suspicious of the activities of national governments and their PTTs is the imperfect nature of some of these markets. Thus, PTTs will often place restrictions on the shared use or resale of private leased lines simply because they are concerned with the effects of foreign competition on the business of local information providers. A further tactic is the imposition of limitations on the number of foreign firms permitted to supply information services in a particular country. Quite apart from the possible retarding effect such practices can have on technological development, they are clearly in restraint of trade. In the long run, they could operate against the national interest of those countries imposing them.

Discriminatory technical standards. In view of the enabling nature of the information technologies, the setting and maintenance of national and international standards for the manufacture and operation of equipment is a highly important matter. Such standards can both help and hinder developments in information markets and, as always, it is the attitude of governments and the PTTs that largely determines the nature of the operating environment. Where technical standards are viewed as a legitimate source of market leverage, either to counter the influence of multinational corporations or in support of local operators, then the result can clearly be the erection of further barriers to trade. An obvious example is the use of different national protocols for the bit sequence of the introductory portion of digitised messages. In some cases, this greatly impairs the efficiency of messages transmitted on foreign equipment, as compared to those transmitted on locally manufactured equipment.[14] Other examples include attempts to amend the existing standards for radio spectrum frequencies to bring them more into line with the requirements of Third World countries, and differences in European and American standards for ISDNs. Clearly, if communication between users is adversely affected by these different national technical standards for equipment, then the long-term interests of both the information industry and the public at large would be served by the harmonisation of technical standards at international level. As is all too obvious, however, there are more than technical considerations at stake.

Privacy and data protection legislation. In the context of barriers to international trade, the same may be said about much of the regulation related to personal privacy and data protection. In trade terms, this became an issue following the enactment of such laws in a number of European countries during the 1970s. Before long, doubts began to surface as to the real purpose of such actions, and nowhere were these questions raised more pointedly than inside large United States multinational corporations. As far as the multinationals were concerned, these laws had less to do with the protection of personal privacy than with the placing of restrictions on the flow of data over international borders.[15] These laws did in fact have a strong basis in fast-growing public and government concern over a wide range of issues related to privacy and data protection. It is equally true, however, that this legislation was a direct result of a growing awareness of the need for some kind of action to enhance the competitive position of the European information industry.[15]

In view of the serious trade imbalance in information goods and services between Europe and its United States and Japanese competitors, such responses are only to be expected. No government or group of governments can be expected to sit back and watch its industries go bankrupt in the face of unrestrained foreign competition, much of it from multinational corporations with political influence to match their awesome economic power. On the other hand, the lesson of economic history is that when protectionism sets in it leads to retaliation, and to events which ultimately impair the workings of the market, with resultant damage to trade. In any case, with its global markets and distance-shattering technologies, the information industry may be a particularly inappropriate vehicle for old-style policies designed to protect and nurture the growth of home industries. Be that as it may, the commercial ethos of the Japanese, and the enduring presence of companies such as IBM, are eloquent testimony to the logic of single-minded self interest, which must on occasion entail the ability to respond in kind to the predatory business methods of overseas rivals. The difficulty lies in deciding where to draw the line between an aggressive commercial stance, backed up with appropriate support at policy level, and the kind of action which would inflict undue damage on the market mechanism.

Although matters of personal privacy might at first appear to be somewhat remote from the concerns of the international information business, it is quite clear that real problems have arisen as a result of the overlap between the two. Burgess is in little doubt as to the rights and wrongs of this situation, arguing that legislation designed to protect personal privacy ought not be allowed to hinder the legitimate and proper transfer of information across national borders.[16] Whereas in principle this is correct, all concerned – governments, the industry and the international community – face very real problems in their attempts to separate corporate from personal matters. Not the least of these is the ease with which personal data, which is raw material for the industry, can be transferred around the world. Inevitably, in the circumstances, those worried about the possible misuse of this information will continue their attempts to control it. Others will exploit such activity for motives of their own. These motives underlie most attempts to interpose barriers between buyer and seller in the information markets of the world.

Artificial barriers in the information market

The erection of trade barriers of any kind poses questions related to transborder dataflow, matters which are considered later in the chapter. However, several issues of particular relevance to dataflows between the advanced information nations are considered at this point. These are: the SWIFT–CEPT controversy, the KDD affair, the new Bundespost regulations, and the European gas pipeline incident.

The SWIFT–CEPT controversy. The protagonists in what was to become a highly significant dispute were the Society for Worldwide Interbank Financial Telecommunications (SWIFT) and the Conference of European Post and Telecommunications Administrations (CEPT). No sooner had the SWIFT network been established, in 1973, as a cheaper and more reliable alternative to established telex channels, than the European PTTs, acting through CEPT, agreed to take collective action against it. The eventual proposals, in 1976, were for new methods of calculating the cost of leased lines, involving both an increased flat-rate charge and an element of volume-sensitivity. In effect, these new charges, which bore little relationship to the actual cost of providing the service, would have threatened the very existence of the SWIFT network.[17]

For all its obvious importance to both sides, the real significance of this dispute was as the first of a series of such actions over the subject of private leased circuits. These problems were aired at the CCITT's Study Group III on the uses of private leased circuits. In May 1978, the CCITT ruled that international private leased circuits should continue to be made available by the PTTs to anybody who needed them.[17] Although this decision removed the immediate threat to the survival of the SWIFT network, it was by no means the end of the story. Problems remain over the matter of tariffs and as to what constitutes the proper use of circuits once they have been leased.

The KDD affair. The matter of private circuits was in evidence once again when, in 1976, the Japanese international telecommunications carrier Kokusai Denshin Denwa (KDD) received a request for leased facilities from two leading United States data processing companies, Control Data Corporation (CDC) and Tymshare, Inc.[17] When, nearly two years later, the

Japanese acceded to these requests, it was only on the basis of certain restrictive conditions. All such operations depend on moving data processing activities between customer terminals and computer centres, depending on the particular function involved. In both cases, however, the Japanese were demanding that the circuit be connected to only a single specified computer system in the United States, and not connected to any American public network. It was also a condition that when a proposed new KDD public data network became available in Japan, the American companies would discuss the possibility of substituting the new facility for their existing leased lines.[17]

These restrictions effectively prevented both the American companies from operating to full effect in the Japanese market. Moreover, being in direct contradiction to established United States trade policies, they eventually attracted the attention of the Department of State. In the event, it required direct negotiations between the respective governments to bring the matter to a satisfactory conclusion. In December 1980, the Japanese Minister of Posts and Telecommunications authorised KDD to negotiate removal of the restrictions. However, as with the SWIFT–CEPT dispute, there are still certain issues to be resolved.[17]

The new Bundespost regulations. The effect of new regulations introduced in 1982 by the German Federal Ministry for Posts and Telecommunications, Bundespost, was similar to that resulting from the KDD restrictions on the use of private leased lines. Specifically, all leased lines entering the Federal Republic must be wired directly to a single terminal device that is not connected to any other communications network in Germany, or must terminate in a computer in Germany that performs true data processing operations on the data transmitted.[17] Compliance with these conditions means that foreign data processing companies are able to access the public networks operated by the Bundespost and, therefore, can do business in Germany. Failure to comply either results in the exclusion of foreign companies from the German market altogether or leaves them subject to much more expensive usage-sensitive charges.

Although such requirements run contrary to both the economic and technological logic of international telecommunications networks, they have much to commend them from the viewpoint of the German data processing industry. However, in the context of global information markets, such actions can only be seen as the erection of further barriers in the way of free trade.

The European gas pipeline incident. Almost without exception, the foregoing restrictions emerged as a response to the dominant world position of the American data processing industry. The affair of the European gas pipeline, on the other hand, involved an attempt by the United States to impose restrictions on those European and Japanese allies engaged on work for the building of a pipeline to carry gas from Siberia in the USSR to Western Europe. The problem developed when, following the imposition of martial law in Poland in December 1981, the United States called upon its allies to join with it in imposing economic sanctions against both Poland and the USSR. The United States had previously expressed concern lest the pipeline development lead to an undesirably high level of European dependence on the USSR. Its allies, on the other hand, were motivated by the commercial opportunities in what was a $15,000 million project. About half of the 6 million tonnes of pipe required for the project was to be supplied by West European countries and most of the remainder by Japan. In addition, Western countries were to supply pipelaying tractors, compressor stations for the maintenance of gas flow, and turbine equipment to propel the gas. Therefore when, in January 1982, sanctions imposed by the United States Government prevented the American General Electric Corporation from supplying some $175 million of turbine parts to European countries, some sort of confrontation became inevitable. In the case of the United Kingdom alone, this embargo put at risk some £200 million in export orders.[18]

The affair rapidly assumed crisis proportions within the western alliance, with the European powers and Japan stubbornly resisting American pressure, and the Americans seeking to introduce even tougher measures. In June 1982 the Americans extended their ban to include not only American companies but also their foreign subsidiaries, and foreign companies manufacturing American-designed components under licence. By this time, the matter had become one of principle, and during June and July, the United Kingdom, France, Germany and Italy all responded to the challenge. In August the United Kingdom Government invoked its Protection of Trading Interests Act, 1980, thus requiring the four leading United Kingdom companies involved to proceed with their contracts regardless of, and if necessary in violation of, the United States embargo.[19] This brought the affair of the gas pipeline to an end.

Although it was a somewhat unusual example, the gas pipeline incident served as further evidence of the vulnerability of international trade to interference. That it can happen again can be inferred not only with reference to such legislation as the United States Export Administration Act, which is designed for that purpose, but also with regard to the existence of COCOM. The innocuously entitled Coordinating Committee on Export Controls was established under the auspices of the North Atlantic Treaty Organisation (NATO) in 1979. Known also as the Coordinating Committee for Exports to Communist Areas, it seeks to operate an embargo through the compilation of lists of strategic materials, which are not to be sold either directly or indirectly by the West to the Eastern bloc countries. An associated body known as CHINCOM is concerned with maintaining a similar embargo against China.

Presumably in such matters, much depends on what is deemed to be of strategic importance and what is not. As happens when questions of security become entangled with the daily business of earning a living, however, the outcome can occasionally be rather different from what was intended. Thus even Switzerland, a country whose name is synonymous with neutrality, has on more than one occasion found itself in conflict with these regulations. Recent cases involving the export of Japanese computer equipment to the USSR have once again called the entire system into question.

Information transfer problems in the developed world

Today, almost any service that can be delivered electronically can be traded. Included in the range of such services are data processing; computer programming; video and audio entertainment; research and development; publishing; advertising; and communication and information services. International trade in services is estimated to be in excess of $600 billion a year.[20] In the circumstances, it is not surprising that the international marketplace for information services is such a hostile place. Nor is this competition restricted to the service industries, with a wide range of industrial corporations heavily dependent upon international telecommunications and data processing facilities. In such a context, therefore, the creation of artificial trade barriers can threaten the future of entire economies, with implications for the providers of computer and communications hardware and software and its related services; the industries which employ these technologies or which use services dependent on them; and the consumers of products and services offered by both groups of enterprises.[21]

The result has been not only a proliferation of information-related issues but also an upsurge of user reaction. This is reflected institutionally in the appearance of these issues before such user-orientated bodies as the OECD. However, users are a vague and amorphous grouping, and opinion is far from unanimous, even on such fundamental issues as private leased lines. Nor is this simply a matter of Europe versus the United States or even of European PTTs against American multinationals. Ranged against both these groups would be a host of smaller companies seeking a toe-hold in the information industry and, therefore, in favour of liberalisation. The large corporate users, however, fearing damage to themselves should the PTTs over-react to such challenges, tend to support the maintenance of controls.

In the developed world, therefore, the picture is one of fragmentation and conflict. The issues concerned can only be properly tackled at an international level, and through the involvement of the whole international community, not just those nations that are currently great information powers. Regulation is inevitable, and it remains only to ensure that it is good rather than bad in its conception and operation.[22] By widening the perspective to include the developing nations, the discussion will take on dimensions that differ in kind as well as in emphasis.

The developing world

Inevitably, in a category that includes most of the nations, races and religions of the world, there can be problems with such generalisations as the 'developing countries'. Even the highly evocative 'Third World', with its images of poverty and backwardness, conceals within it an immense diversity. By such means are least developed countries such as Chad and Niger lumped along with oil-rich states like Saudi Arabia or Kuwait, or with fast-industrialising nations such as Mexico and Brazil.[23]

There is also a tendency to equate conditions in all developing countries with those in the very poorest nations, in countries which have yet to achieve an agricultural revolution let alone come to grips with the problems of industrialisation. Blighted by low incomes and low levels of literacy, and with a very small share of their GDP derived from manufacturing, these are the countries which help to create the Third World stereotype. They include such places as Afghanistan, Bangladesh, Haiti, and the Central African Republic.[24] On the other hand, there are the newly industrialised countries (NICs), where, in places such as Hong Kong, Singapore, Taiwan, and South Korea, there has been spectacular economic growth, often involving exploitation of the latest technologies.[25]

The problems of the developing countries are clearly of a different order from anything encountered in the rich nations of the North. While the developed countries are no strangers to problems of poverty and unemployment, these pale into insignificance beside the misery endured by the shanty town dwellers of Rio de Janeiro or Mexico City, or by the landless peasants of the Indian subcontinent. These examples were chosen deliberately because each of these countries has undergone a considerable degree of industrialisation. Unfortunately, most of this industrialisation has occurred apart from mainstream developments in society, leaving the basic socioeconomic structures largely unaffected. Also, there has been insufficient scope for the emergence of viable service sectors.[26]

Therefore, the majority of developing countries face an enormous task in their efforts to achieve a measure of industrialisation, let alone of informatisation. Whether the goal is the building of an indigenous manufacturing capability or the modernisation of existing industrial capacity in pursuit of information-led growth, the role of information and its associated technologies will be crucial. Unfortunately, on top of all its other problems, the South suffers from an information famine.[3]

Although the European gas pipeline affair provides ample illustration of the inherent vulnerability of any market to external political pressures, the indications are that in developing countries the impact of noncommercial factors is all the more potent. Poverty and a continued dependence on both natural elements and powerful outside forces are reason enough for the absence of indigenous manufacturing and service sectors. However, in what are often highly traditional societies, the presence of certain social and religious values constitutes another set of relevant factors. Central to an understanding of these 'environmental' influences are the related issues of ideology, sovereignty and informatics.

The importance of ideology

In the West, ideology tends to be associated with those one-party states and ultra-authoritarian regimes of the developing world and the Eastern bloc. The fact is, however, that no country or group of countries is immune from some form of ideological influence. Neither Marxists nor mullahs have a monopoly on the subject, and a climate of unrestrained free enterprise can be as obnoxious in traditional societies as one characterised by regimentation and control would be in the relatively relaxed surroundings of most Western democracies.

A particularly relevant example of such ideological differences can be seen in conflicting approaches to the treatment of information. Thus in the North the emphasis tends to be upon what could basically be termed a 'human rights' approach. Information is perceived as a fundamental human right and its availability and transmission an element essential to the operation and survival of a free society. In the South, on the other hand, the tendency is for matters of information to be treated within a 'rights of nations' context. In essence, this is interpreted as the inalienable right of independent countries to protect themselves and their citizens from injury and misrepresentation at home and abroad.[27] In practice this can mean that the free flow of information and ideas deemed so essential to the Western way of life is, in emerging countries, a matter which takes second place to the wider national interest. As will be seen below, this basic difference in attitudes to information, and to its wider role in society, has implications both for the development process itself and for that entire structure of international relations upon which ultimately everything else depends. A further indication of the role which information factors have come to play in such developments is their growing importance to the issue of national sovereignty.

The importance of sovereignty

Sovereignty is a concept long established in international law and hitherto interpreted as the supreme, absolute and uncontrollable power by which any independent state is governed.[28] However, the revolutionary impact of the new information technology, and mounting evidence of its abuse, have led to calls for a reconsideration of the entire operation and scope of the concept. Two examples, both related to satellite technology, should suffice to indicate the validity of these concerns. First, there is nothing to prevent developed countries from using remote earth-sensing to acquire unauthorised knowledge about mineral and other resources in developing countries. Quite apart from commercial and strategic considerations, this is a clear intrusion on the rights and territories of those nations subjected to the practice. Second, there is the threat implicit in the power of direct broadcast satellites. Using these systems, it is possible to transmit direct to viewers in another country, with the possibility of offence either on grounds of programme content or of 'spillover', that is interference with local transmissions.

In the circumstances, it is hardly surprising that many countries are genuinely worried about the implications of such developments for their national sovereignty. Demands are growing for the recognition of national rights in information. If agreed by the international community, these would extend beyond the terrestrial domain to embrace information activities in the vast reaches of outer space. The increasing importance of sovereignty underlies the growing interest in informatics and, in particular, in the formulation of national informatics policies.

The importance of informatics

For many developing countries the quest for self-sufficiency in communications and data processing technologies is fuelled not just by the demands of national pride but also by a desire to change a relationship which is basically one of exploitation. As in days gone by, when the developed countries plundered the developing world for supplies of raw materials, then later sold them back at enhanced prices in the form of finished goods, so it is today with the raw material of the information age, unprocessed data.[29] The problem is of course that there is often not a great deal that can be done, at least in the short term. One way forward could lie in exploitation of the potential social and economic benefits of informatics. Bortnik has claimed that informatics facilitates development at three levels. First, it fosters economic development by providing access to information and its associated technologies. Second, it facilitates social development through the processes of education and the transmission and preservation of cultural values. Finally, it contributes to political development by virtue of its input to, and support for, the decision-making process.[29]

In support of these assertions, Bortnik has cited the celebrated example of Brazil, a country whose experience in this field has led to its becoming something of a spokesman on informatics matters for developing countries. Brazilian informatics activities date back to the 1970s and realisation of the importance of computer technology both to long-term development prospects and to the immediate balance of payments situation. The Coordinating Committee on Data Processing Activities (CAPRE) had its brief extended in 1976 from one of overseeing the purchase and use of all computers and related equipment in Brazil to one of future responsibility for the production of a national informatics plan. This farsighted and imaginative policy left little to chance, and it is easy to understand its attractions for other developing countries. In addition to laying down criteria for the import of equipment, which included such requirements as export potential, the transfer of technology and the establishment of local control, it simply made it impossible to process Brazilian data outside the country unless it could be shown that indigenous data processing facilities were unable to do the job.[29]

So important was the function which CAPRE came to perform that, in 1979, it was replaced by another body, which became part of the National Security Council and reported to the President himself. This Special Informatics Agency (SEI) was charged with two major objectives: the development of national telecommunications and computer industries, and the regulation of transborder dataflows in the interests of national sovereignty and economic growth.[29]

Problems of North–South information exchange

This final section of the chapter will look at some of the specific points of conflict that have arisen in the area of international information transfer. Significantly these are all notable sources of friction between North and South, and should they be allowed to continue unchecked then the consequences for international relations could be extremely serious. These problem areas are allocation of the radiofrequency spectrum, technology transfer, transborder dataflow, and the 'free flow' versus 'New World Information and Communication Order' controversy.

Allocation of the radiofrequency spectrum

Although the allocation of radiofrequencies between countries on the basis of need would seem to be essentially a technical operation, there is in fact rather more to it than this. Indeed, the reason why frequency allocation is a source of major conflict between North and South is that the international information arena has become just one more venue for political confrontation. This is not to deny that there are very real issues at stake. Nevertheless, whatever the justification for their attempts to bring about a re-allocation of frequencies, the developing countries have been motivated by largely nontechnical considerations.

The body which attempts to settle such disputes, on the basis of voluntary agreement, is the International Telecommunications Union (ITU). From the viewpoint of the developed nations, who until recently dominated its proceedings, there is much to be said for adherence to existing arrangements. This means that any country seeking either frequency allocations or slots in the geostationary orbit, submits its requirements for consideration by an International Frequency Registration Board (IFRB). This system, claim the developed countries, is both fair and efficient. It allocates slots and frequencies as required and allows for the operation of technical change, by which process in any case the need for rationing will ultimately be made redundant.[30] Seen from the perspective of the developing countries, on the other hand, this sounds suspiciously like an expression of self interest. It also seems geared to the maintenance of a status quo in which those countries which are most in need of advanced telecommunications systems are very much the minority shareholders in the existing network of world telecommunications facilities. Hence, they would argue, what is needed is a more equitable allocation of both radiofrequencies and orbital slots among all the nations of the world.[30]

There is clearly something to be said for both these viewpoints. On grounds of technical efficiency and commonsense, there is little to be gained from allocating facilities to countries in response to emotional appeals which have little to do with either current technical capacity or likely prospects for development. From the perspective of those who feel excluded from the present system, however, this is no way at all to consider the allocation of a scarce natural resource, the benefits of which should be available to all mankind. Whatever the logic or, indeed, the justice of the case, the signs are that neither technological arguments nor those based on an appeal to principle will be likely to carry the day. Political realities may well be decisive, and few things in life are more unpredictable than politics.

From the standpoint of the developing nations, however, there are already some signs of progress. Where once the developed countries were in the majority at the ITU, they are now outnumbered two to one by Third World countries, and in some ways this is beginning to tell. Hence the World Administrative Radio Conference (WARC) in 1979 adopted a motion that those countries having unused allocations should be required to relinquish them for possible re-allocation. The ITU conference of 1985 produced a further concession from the advanced nations. In future, countries may be able to stake a claim to certain radio frequencies and orbital positions even though they may not as yet be intending to put satellites into orbit.[31]

Nevertheless, it would be in nobody's interest if the discussion of such important technological issues was to become simply an appendage of the ritual verbal conflict between North and South. Otherwise, the circumstances which led to the withdrawal of the United Kingdom and the United States from Unesco could be repeated, with unhelpful consequences for the development process.

Technology transfer

One feature upon which all concerned would claim to agree is the importance of transferring technology and expertise from North to South. What is often understated, however, is the fact that technology transfer is a highly complex process that involves, among other things, both donor and receiver, the nature of their relationship and of the technology concerned, and certain minimal preconditions for success. To be meaningful, the technology transfer process must include not just the technology itself but also the training and support facilities that will enable the receiving country to sustain the impact following the initial infusion of resources.[31] As Rada has shown, however, most of the evidence for success in such ventures comes from within the developed world, and involves operation of a threefold mechanism: mobility of personnel, who take their knowledge with them; second sourcing, or the agreement between two companies to manufacture fully compatible products; and cross-licensing agreements based on a mutual exchange of technology.[32]

As for the technology itself, considerable difficulties can arise in the wake of attempts to import equipment and facilities that are simply inappropriate to the circumstances of the developing country concerned. The risks of this happening are increasing all the time with the onset of what Rada has termed 'disembodied technology'. This means that the technology comes with a considerable amount of inbuilt information, much of which is laden with the cultural codes of the developed world. Accordingly, when imported into a developing country lacking the necessary indigenous support skills, it simply creates an illusion of technology transfer and results only in increased dependence.[32] As a consequence of such difficulties, Unesco has recommended that sufficient attention be paid to the adoption of technologies which are more appropriate, in that they are labour intensive, smaller scale and more harmonious in both cultural and ecological terms. The problem, as Unesco readily concedes, is that existing information networks are global in scale and require an ability to meet sophisticated operating standards.[33] Appropriate or otherwise, the business of technology transfer seems set to be a laborious and protracted affair. Moreover, it is difficult to escape the conclusion that in many cases it will be a matter of travelling hopefully with little real prospect of arriving.

For those developing countries whose prospects of advancement are more encouraging, there remain certain preconditions for the effective transfer of knowledge from more technologically advanced societies. These include a widespread awareness of the value of information for development, and a level of indigenous organisation capable of supporting the nascent information transfer process. Also included would be a range of infrastructure improvements necessary to support the systems and the services to be based upon them.[33] The problem is that in the absence of such broad based improvements, which in themselves represent a considerable degree of social, economic and cultural development, the process of technology transfer seems likely to be doomed before it can even begin to take shape. Nevertheless, the evident interest in informatics plans, coupled with the emergence of developing nations in all the leading information fora of the world, suggests that the battle for awareness is well on the way to being won. The matter of infrastructure improvements could prove to be much more critical, in view of the resource implications involved. Even more problematical, in terms of that home market so essential for the support of an indigenous information industry, is the creation of sufficient wealth to stimulate the demand for information goods and services. Given that informatisation follows development, and not the other way round, this remains a great imponderable. Nevertheless, even Rada, to whom informatisation implies the incorporation of greater amounts of knowledge and information into goods and services, admits the possibility that for a minority of developing countries, opportunities exist in the fast-expanding international services sector.[34] Clearly, for these opportunities to be realised would be an excellent example of successful technical transfer.

Transborder dataflow

Although from time immemorial data and information have been crossing and recrossing international borders, the sheer scale of the process today, and the speed at which it operates, have created an entirely new set of challenges for the international community. Quintessentially a product of the information age, the issue of transborder dataflow touches on many of the topics already identified as critical to information transfer, including sovereignty, the free flow of information, privacy, the protection of native industries, and recognition of information as a key national resource.[35] Brought to its present proportions by the convergence of telecommunications and data processing technologies, transborder dataflow can be defined as the electronic transmission of data across political boundaries for processing or storage in computer files or both.[35]

Although dependent on the enabling characteristics of the new information technologies, the current manifestation of transborder dataflow also owes its growth to the presence of certain social and commercial factors. These include the growth and subsequent internationalisation of trade in information goods and services; the expansion of world trade and, in particular, the globalisation of such information-intensive industries as banking and insurance, tourism and air transport; and the growth of large multinational corporations.[36] The world is criss-crossed by high-speed telecommunications networks, publicly and privately operated, moving vast quantities of data on a 24-hour basis between different time zones – dataflows which include everything from seat reservations to stock exchange prices to criminal records. This global dataflow process is, in essence, one vast international network marketplace. In effect it is a high technology entrepôt, with multiplier effects on trade and development. It is a key issue in North–South information exchange, although in fact most countries, rich or poor, have a negative information trade balance with the United States.[37] As a result, there are problems, some caused directly by the dataflow process, others the outcome of attempts to bring it under control.

The major problems directly associated with transborder dataflow have already been covered in one way or another and are reiterated here simply on grounds of completeness. In essence, these relate to the difficulties facing nations in the spheres of sovereignty and vulnerability, often leading to legal problems in such areas as privacy and data protection, copyright and intellectual property. Of particular relevance to the developing nations are problems stemming from the international division of labour and the structure of the international data market. Basically this concerns the deleterious effects of exporting data for processing in the advanced countries. This can adversely affect local infrastructures and capacities in the emerging nations, and can lead to increased dependence, with key decision-making functions affected by data located on foreign soil.[38]

Indirect problems relate mainly to those defensive measures initiated by governments against what they perceive to be the threats posed by transborder dataflow. One obvious example of such reaction has been the enactment of privacy and data protection laws, another has been the inclusion of transborder dataflow within the provisions of national informatics plans. Whereas such protection has been necessary, there is always the danger of this kind of legislation going too far. Mahon has raised the spectre of a cycle of action and reaction, with data protection escalating to become data overprotection, leading to the possibility of offshore havens for those who wish to evade the restrictions of data protection and intellectual copyright codes.[39] Similarly there is concern in business circles about the kinds of restrictions placed upon multinational companies doing business in countries such as Brazil. There, any proposals for the import of equipment or the export of data are subject to the most stringent controls, involving disclosure of company information and objectives, and, where necessary, the establishment of duplicate data-processing facilities in Brazil. The presence of such requirements adds greatly to the cost of doing business and can lead to inbuilt inefficiencies that would not be tolerated in less regulated environments.[40]

The benefits of transborder dataflow can be seen at both the general and specific levels. In general terms, the development of an international market for information goods and services provides clear stimulus to the overall expansion of world trade. In more specific terms, the flow of data across national borders supports the process of technology transfer and with it the movement of people and ideas. As Mahon points out, in respect of the European Community, regulations on public calls for tender almost guarantee transborder dataflows, while there is already copyright law for the international protection of rights.[41] Also, although the reverse situation is more often mentioned, transborder dataflow can help to reduce barriers between countries and increase international understanding.

Finally, transborder dataflow has the potential to help in at least three different directions. First, by giving users instant access to a rapidly expanding and diversifying pool of up-to-date knowledge, dataflows can help redress the imbalance between developed and developing nations, while also enabling the latter to improve the management of local resources. Second, where the local branches of multinational corporations have access to advanced technologies, they may use this to enhance overall national competitiveness in international markets. Last, by providing access to the considerable amount of data about developing countries held on the international market, transborder dataflow could become a useful tool for economic cooperation between developing countries themselves.[42]

There is a clear need for some form of international agreement on transborder dataflow. Indeed, the matter has already attracted the attention of such organisations as the Council of Europe, the IBI and the OECD. The Council of Europe's response has been to issue a convention, or set of guidelines, seeking to ensure some commonality of approach to dataflow problems by the European nations.[43] The IBI has set up international working parties to examine, among other things, the economic and commercial impact of transborder dataflow and the international environment for this. These IBI working parties are controversial, seeking to confront some of the more obvious issues of sovereignty and equity that exist between the developed and the developing countries. Their programme includes consideration of an outline universal data protection instrument, which, if it were to obtain international recognition, would standardise rights and responsibilities in transborder dataflows.[43] The OECD issued guidelines on transborder dataflow in 1981. These outline the interests of member states, while recognising the often contradictory nature of an environment that at one and the same time contains demands for the free flow of information and for the recognition of rights such as privacy. These guidelines also reiterate the need for coordinated international action on a subject that, in addition to the organisations cited as examples, has attracted the attention of others such as the GATT, the ITU, and Unesco.[43] The very universality of the problems involved makes the search for some kind of concerted approach all the more difficult.

Whatever happens over transborder dataflow, it will not happen quickly. The subject is much too complex and controversial to allow quick and easy solutions. In the meantime, individual nations are busy devising their own unilateral responses, such as the proposed use of 'gateways' for the systematic channelling of data in and out of Brazil.[44] Indeed, the French are reported to have developed a system for the imposition of customs duties and value-added taxes on dataflows, which can distinguish between public and private data, and between that which is saleable and that which is not.[45] However, as Mahon points out, in seeking the necessary compromise between sensible regulation and freedom to trade, policy makers should bear in mind the relative ease with which controls can be circumvented.[46]

The New World Information and Communication Order (NWICO)

Of all the issues between the developed and the developing nations, few are more comprehensive and, seemingly, intractable than those arising from different attitudes to the NWICO. This dispute is essentially ideological, the product of two very different ways of looking at the world. The developing world's perspective on the NWICO has been expressed by Hamelink as:

> the international exchange of information, in which nations which develop their cultural system in an autonomous way, and with complete sovereign control of resources, fully and effectively participate as independent members of the international community.[47]

There seems to be little in this description likely to cause offence. Nevertheless, the reality of North–South relations on this matter tells a very different story, and one indeed made quite explicit by a simple change of definition. Hence, Masmoudi, one of its chief proponents, has described the NWICO in the following terms:

> The New World Information Order, founded on democratic principles, seeks to establish relations of equality in the communication field between developed and developing nations, and aims at greater justice and greater balance. Far from calling in question the freedom of information, it proposes to ensure that this principle is applied fairly and equitably for all nations, and not only in the case of the more developed among them.[48]

It is clear that this statement, and associated calls for a new international economic order, would find far from universal favour in the West. Not that the NWICO can be blamed for what, after all, is a clash of ideologies, its own and those underpinning Western advocacy of the free flow of information. In the West, the NWICO and its associated proposals for control are viewed as a threat to press freedom and hence to freedom of thought and action. In defence of such principles, a group of journalists and others, convened in France in 1981, issued the Declaration of Talloires.[49]

In this ideological struggle, two consistent targets for developing countries have been the United Nations Declaration of Freedom of Information, 1946 and the Universal Declaration of Human Rights, 1948.[49] The former laid down that all states should proclaim policies by which the free flow of information, within countries and across frontiers, would be protected. The Universal Declaration of Human Rights reinforced these 'freedom of information' statements by declaring that everyone had the right to freedom of opinion and expression, including freedom to hold opinions and to see, receive and impart information and ideas through any media and regardless of frontiers.[50]

In the West the attacks have been generally deplored as endangering the very fabric of democracy. In this case, moreover, it is 'West' rather than 'North', because the Eastern bloc is aligned with the Third World on these issues. The very fact of Soviet and East European involvement is sufficient to convince many Western observers of the underlying threat to freedom contained in the NWICO proposals. Again, the absence of anything remotely resembling a free press, and the blatant imposition of all kinds of censorship in many of those countries pressing for a change, are scarcely calculated to engender confidence in opponents of the measures proposed.

From the viewpoint of many developing countries, on the other hand, such observations would seem dangerously overloaded with Western values. At one level, this involves differing perspectives on information, which, claims, Masmoudi, must be viewed as a social good and as a cultural product, and not as a material commodity or as merchandise.[51] At the more general level of international relations, Masmoudi has identified four areas of immediate concern to developing countries. First is the major imbalance of information flows, which are heavily weighted in favour of the developed countries. Second is the control exercised by the developed nations over all forms of information, including the allocation of radiofrequencies. Third, there is the de facto perpetuation of colonialism, through operation of the current system of information flow. Fourth, the fact that the developed nations have a virtual monopoly of world communications means that they can broadcast exactly what they choose, and that, as a result, only stereotyped and sensational images of the developing countries are transmitted in the international media.[51]

Despite the existence of such deeply held opinions, publication in 1981 of the report of the International Commission for the Study of Communication Problems led to considerable criticism of the NWICO principles. Entitled *Many voices, one world* but known universally as the Macbride Report, after its author, the celebrated Irish jurist Sean Macbride, this turned out to be a battleground for opposing ideologies, East and West.[52] Inevitably, there were misunderstandings and, ironic in the circumstances, failures of communication Hence Macbride's insistence that the NWICO was a generalised process, aiming to improve the lot of mankind as a whole, was overlooked in a welter of recriminations over issues of press freedom and the free flow of information. The fact was that out of a total of 82 recommendations for action, the Macbride Report contained only 11 that were directly applicable to the work of journalists. Again, while some of its recommendations were undoubtedly biased against the Western media, these weaknesses may have been used to obscure other important proposals.[53] Among examples of these more positive proposals were three subsequently cited by Suprenant: encouragement of national book publication and distribution; preference to be given to noncommercial forms of mass communication; and all involved in the media to contribute to the fulfilment of human rights in the spirit of the Unesco declaration on the mass media, the Helsinki Final Act, and the International Bill of Human Rights.[53]

While the inclusion of such recommendations would in itself be no guarantee of the libertarian credentials of the NWICO, not least owing to the continued existence of the 11 offending clauses, it must be remembered that politics is the art of the possible. It is unlikely that any series of recommendations on any subject of major international concern would be completely acceptable to all interested parties. By the same token, those who are pressing for adoption of the NWICO must understand that if the one world of its title is to mean anything then many voices must be heard, and not just those which are currently acceptable in the developing world.

Summary

In bringing this chapter to a close, it remains only to emphasise the essential unity of the various issues given separate consideration within it. The economic, social, political and cultural implications of information transfer are matters of truly global significance, requiring global responses based upon cooperation and compromise. Although the North enjoys almost all the advantages in its dealings with the poorer and less developed South, the relationship between them is complex and changing. Of obvious importance is the mutual interest in the social and economic development of the South, upon which the future economic prosperity and, indeed, security of the North in increasing measure depend.

As for the development problems of the developing world, there are clear indications that the transfer of information and technology could help in the build up of indigenous expertise and infrastructures. This process is under way in a variety of forms, including bilateral arrangements between states, and a wide range of programmes operated under the auspices of international agencies. Unesco has maintained a persistent interest in such matters, not just through its General Information Programme (PGI) but also by offering help in the field of technology transfer. There is a continuing problem of funding for the United Nations and its agencies, however, and in any case the answer might best come from arrangements which involve more of an element of self-help. The possibility of developing nations joining together in common self-interest has already been demonstrated through their modest but definite successes at the ITU. Proposals for a shared satellite communication system for developing countries, especially if founded on the development of common communication protocols for network interface, would represent a giant step forward for mankind. In the meantime there remain the more mundane but nonetheless critically important problems of stimulating wider awareness of information, and ensuring adequate use of existing information resources in the developing countries.

Finally, it is in everybody's interests that the information transfer process be nurtured and developed. The 'One World' adumbrated in the Macbride Report is already a fact of life, albeit in a form very different from that which many in the South would want to see. Somehow or other, those in the North who support free flow must come to understand that this is actually a cultural matter, and that in propagating the Western view they are seen by many in the South to be threatening indigenous values. Even viewed from a European perspective, free flow takes on a rather different meaning when one is on the receiving end, faced with both cultural inundation and economic domination. The changes which many countries, North and South, would regard as necessary, will only come about through negotiation, a process in which the interdependence of the two worlds will become all the more evident. With the development gap between North and South widening all the time, especially in the critically important sphere of information and communications technologies, this is no time for ideological rigidity. The nations of the world must decide either to work together and share the benefits of new technology or, by retreating further into worlds of mutual suspicion and mistrust, to risk destroying everything.

References

1. Narasimhan, R., The socioeconomic significance of information technology to developing countries, *The Information Society Journal*, 2, 1, 1985, 65–79.
2. Intergovernmental Bureau of Informatics, *IBI, informatics and the concert of nations: simultaneous growth*, Rome, IBI, 1985, 17.
3. Fyson, Nancy Lui, *The development puzzle*, 7th edn, London, Hodder & Stoughton, 1984, 1.
4. Nora, Simon and Alain Minc, *The computerisation of society: a report to the President of France*, Cambridge, Massachusetts, MIT Press, 1980.
5. Canadian Department of Communications, *Consultative Committee on the Implications of Telecommunications for Canadian Sovereignty*, 1979. (The Clyne Report.)
6. Commission of the European Communities, *European society faced with the challenge of the new information technologies*, Luxembourg, European Commission, 1979. (The Dublin Report.)
7. Ramsey, Thomas J., Europe responds to the challenge of the new information technologies: a teleinformatics strategy for the 1980s, *Cornell International Law Journal*, 14, 1981, 237–85.
8. Martyn, John, *Information industry involvements of the European Community*, London, British Library, 1985. (R&D Report 5852.)
9. Large, Peter, *The Guardian*, Friday, 14 October 1986, 26.
10. Sutherland, Ewan, 'Telecommunications: policy issues and regulatory practices affecting the future'. Proceedings of the Salzburg Seminar, Session 243, 1985. Unpublished.
11. Burgess, B. C., Restrictions on the transfer and use of international information. Paper presented at the ITU/American Bar Association World Forum, San Francisco, 1981.
12. Feketekuty, Geza and Jonathon D. Aronson, Restrictions on trade in communications and information services, *The Information Society Journal*, 2, 3/4, 1984, 217–33.
13. Burgess, op. cit., 10.
14. Feketekuty and Aronson, op. cit., 223.
15. Bushkin, Arthur A., The uses of technology: the new battleground in world trade. Paper presented at the Annual Institute on World Affairs, Ames, Iowa, 1983.
16. Burgess, op. cit., 7.
17. Markoski, Joseph P., Telecommunications regulations as barriers to the transborder flow of information, *Cornell International Law Journal*, 14, 1981, 287–331.
18. *Keesing's Contemporary Archives*, 30 April 1982.
19. Ibid., 24 September 1982.
20. Feketekuty, Geza and Kathryn Hauser, The impact of information technology on trade in services. Offprint, details not yet available.
21. Burgess, op. cit., 5.
22. Eger, John, The global phenomenon of teleinformatics: an introduction, *Cornell International Law Journal*, 14, 1981, 203–36.

23. Keren, Carl and Larry Harmon, Information services industries in less developed countries, in *Annual review of information science & technology*, ed. M. E. Williams, vol. 17, White Plains, New York, Knowledge Industry Publications, 1980, 289–324.
24. Fyson, op. cit., 2.
25. O'Brien, Sean, Information, information technology and the developing world. Masters dissertation for the Department of Information Studies, The Queen's University of Belfast, 1986, 5. Unpublished.
26. Narasimhan, op. cit., 73.
27. Suprenant, Thomas T., Global threats to information, in *Annual review of information science & technology*, ed. M. E. Williams, vol. 20, White Plains, New York, Knowledge Industry Publications, 1985, 3–25.
28. Eger, op. cit., 231.
29. Bortnik, Jane, International information flows: the developing world perspective, *Cornell International Law Journal*, 14, 1981, 340.
30. Suprenant, op. cit., 8.
31. O'Brien, op. cit., 75.
32. Rada, Juan, Information technology and the Third World, in *The information technology revolution*, ed. Tom Forrester, Oxford, Blackwell, 1985, 571–89.
33. Keren and Harmon, op. cit., 298.
34. Rada, op. cit., 588.
35. Suprenant, op. cit., 15.
36. Transnational corporations and transborder dataflows, in *Information, economics and power*, ed. R. Cruise-O'Brien, London, Hodder & Stoughton, 1983, 42–69.
37. Martyn, John, *The U.K. information industry: current issues, 5. Transborder dataflow*, London, British Library, 1985, 1.
38. Bortnik, op. cit., 339.
39. Mahon, Barry, Transborder dataflow (TBDF) and how it impinges on the information industry, *Aslib Proceedings*, 38, 8, August 1986, 257–61.
40. Bortnik, op. cit., 343.
41. Mahon, op. cit., 259.
42. Cruise-O'Brien, op. cit., 59.
43. Eger, op. cit., 209.
44. Bortnik, op. cit., 342.
45. Eger, op. cit., 223.
46. Mahon, op. cit., 260.
47. Hamelink, Cees, ed., *Communication in the eighties: a reader on the Macbride Report*, Rome, IDOC International, 1980, 185.
48. Masmoudi, Mustapha, The New World Information Order, *Journal of Communication*, 29, 2, Spring 1979, 175–85.
49. Talloires, France, *Voices of Freedom Conference*, 15–17 May 1981.
50. Bortnik, op. cit., 345.
51. Masmoudi, op. cit., 175–85.
52. Macbride, Sean, *Many voices, one world: towards a more just and efficient world information and communication order*, New York, UNIPUB, 1980.
53. Suprenant, op. cit., 12.

CHAPTER 10

Information policy

In more than one sense this chapter on information policy marks the culmination of this book. Many of the issues arising in the course of previous chapters were seen to have policy implications and they appear again here within a policy context. More fundamentally, however, if information is anything like as important to society as this book has made out, a chapter on information policy could provide a fitting and, indeed, necessary conclusion to the work. As in the case of previous chapters, what follows is intended more as an introduction to the subject than a comprehensive study of information policy. This in itself is challenge enough in an area as diffuse and ambiguous as to comprise at one level all the activities of government and at the other, specific rulings on ownership of, and access to, intellectual property.

The need for information policy

Although the need for some kind of policy or policies to deal with information-related issues becomes most apparent as and when they arise, there are deeper, underlying reasons why the information factor should be a matter of concern to policy makers. First, there are those changes in the economy and in society that have been reported in preceding chapters – changes involving the convergence not just of technologies but also of functions and jurisdictions. Where once it was a relatively simple matter to determine which organisations were responsible for, say, broadcasting or the telephone service, it is no longer quite so clear cut. Thus, observed Rosenberg, as confusion over jurisdiction increased, so the need for policies to deal with it also increased.[1] Second, there is the influence of technological change itself – something that has proved to be every bit as much a source of enablement in social and economic terms as it has been in technological terms. Obvious examples are the impact of miniaturisation and digitisation upon the telecommunications industry, and their implications for the emergence of value-added information services. The inevitable conflict of new and old technologies, and of established and emerging interests, resulted not just in attempts to explain what was happening but also in a search for compromise in the shape of public policy making.[2] Third, that the result was policies directed not just at science or at information technology but at a wider, much more diffuse area, was a reflection of the perceived importance of information to the national interest in countries all over the world. As was stated in the official United States submission to an OECD conference on information, computer and communications policy in 1980, it is the ability of information to change relationships between nations, people and organisations which has given it a more pronounced and, therefore, more important role in society.[3] As this role grows even more significant with the emergence of information societies, the need to plan and provide for the information factor could well become the central focus of national policy. If this sounds somewhat utopian, there is always the example of Japan to remind us of both the benefits of information policy and the dangers of underestimating its importance. With reference to what he termed 'informationalization', that is the conscious utilisation of information in industry, international relations, the home and the wider society, Kawahata has shown both what has already been done and what is in prospect for that most information-conscious of societies.[4] Although Japan may be atypical in the extent to which it has developed and pursued its information policies, its experience seems to be the clearest vindication to date of the need for them.

What is information policy?

Although the question might appear more than usually rhetorical, it is well worth asking in view of the ambiguities inherent both in the concept of policy and in its practical applications. Hence there is policy in the sense of a broad general plan of action to be adopted by an organisation or government, for example national economic policy, or, more narrowly, there are policies which in effect are a series of guidelines on specific topics or in discrete areas, such as science policy or information technology policy. Such policies can be enacted by the legislature or the courts or emerge from international organisations and regulatory bodies such as PTTs. In many cases, there will be conflicts of interest over aspects of information policy both within and between countries. Frequently this will take the form of disputes between publicly funded organisations and those within the private sector, with additional difficulties arising out of the inadequacy or inappropriateness of domestic information policy for what are often the very different circumstances of international information transactions. Yet again, there can be differences of interpretation, with information policy variously perceived in relation to the development of library and information services, or the management and control of information within government or, again, the protection or enhancement of national resources or sovereignty.

Whereas this chapter takes the wider perspective on information policy, it must acknowledge the difficulties arising from relationships between the more specific elements. Thus, while viewing information policy in terms of society's response to a range of information-related problems and of the satisfaction of information and other needs, it must come to terms with a plethora of often unstated, and usually uncoordinated, policies to do with science, scientific information and information technology and, of course, information. An obvious source of difficulty, as pointed out by Brown in a United Kingdom context, is that whereas information technology policy enjoys the benefits of having a discrete area of application, the making of information policy is much more difficult, with the subject so diffuse as to defy delegation to any single department of government.[5] One result of this situation has been a tendency to overemphasise the technological aspects of the information policy arena, leading to the kind of criticism that, in the United Kingdom, followed publication of the Alvey Report, namely that information was being overlooked in the rush to develop new technologies. In the event such imbalances tend to even out, not least because there are other elements in the process, other interest groups seeking to be heard.

In any case, the enabling characteristics of the technology would give it a major if not decisive role in policy formulation, with in many cases access to the technology determining who can send or receive information, under what conditions and at what price. It was on such grounds that Bushkin and Yurow, authors of the United States information policy submission to the 1980 OECD seminar, advised against any attempt to separate policies dealing with information technology from those about information itself, maintaining that the ultimate concern should be with the overall consequences of the policy rather than with questions or policies relating to a particular technology.[6] This seems to be good advice and very much in line with the approach taken in this chapter. The purpose of information policy is enhancement of the general welfare through the widest possible diffusion of the benefits of information and its associated technologies throughout the economy and society. Such ends are likely to be best served by the creation of wide-ranging and flexible information policies capable of accommodating the often conflicting demands of economic efficiency and social equity, free information flow and wider national interests.

Quite clearly, therefore, one is talking about a collective concept, about a set of policies rather than one single, comprehensive statement. In fact, this is a recurring theme in the literature of the subject, with commentators as far apart as Australia, Western Europe and the United States all stressing the collective nature of the policy-making process. Hence, the Arthur D. Little discussion document on information policy in the Netherlands used the plural form to describe information policies as those which laid down the central ground rules for the participation of the country, its people, its businesses and institutions in information-related activities at both the national and international level.[7] As to the range of these information activities, a symposium held in the same country two years later described information policies as those concerned with dissemination of research results; subsidising and stimulating the information industries; broadcasting, tele-communications, libraries and archives; organisation of governmental information resources; public information activities; and computer and information literacy.[8]

The very spread of interests and activities involved emphasises both the importance of these information issues and the urgency of the need for action on the policy front. It also indicates something of the difficulties facing the policy makers, who could well turn out to be more effective in a coordinating and facilitating role rather than as the originators of radical statements of information policy. Even where more active courses of action are contemplated, the need is very much for a pragmatic and piecemeal approach which relates the ideal to the possible. At a recent British Library seminar on the subject, the major tasks in any approach to policy formulation were enumerated as identification of those areas in which the policy maker actually has the power to change things; assessment of the level and type of any political inputs required; and the placing of policy issues within a wider political, social and economic context.[9] Attention will now turn to the policy-making process itself, with the emphasis thereafter on the general or national level of policy making.

The policy-making process

Although the policy-making process will vary according to the needs and conditions of different countries, there is sufficient common ground in the matter of overall objectives to permit a certain amount of generalisation. Apart from the elements of the process itself, the main points for consideration concern the structures for information policy making and the major participants involved in the process.

Elements in the policy-making process

In calling for a practical approach to the formulation of national information policies, Tocatlian recognised as a prerequisite for success the identification of the information requirements of society. He also designated as essential to the elaboration of any such policy two further developments: devising means to ensure that these information requirements are met, and promotion of the effective use of information resources.[10] Even for advanced industrial nations with highly developed information infrastructures, these conditions would be by no means easily satisfied, and in some respects compliance could be easier for those emerging nations with clearly identified national development goals.

Whatever the levels of development involved, realisation of any of these requirements would itself entail facing up to a series of policy decisions. Hence, identification goes beyond the simple recognition of need to the making of choices over the degree of priority to be afforded to various user groups and the different modes of service delivery. The satisfaction of national information requirements entails the resolution of policy issues across the spectrum of information generation, storage, retrieval and dissemination, notably in such areas as infrastructure development, conditions of access and the provision of resources of all kinds. The promotion of information use remains, in many cases, the most intractable problem of all, with obvious policy implications in the spheres of information literacy and user education.[10] Quite apart from the complexity of such decisions, their resource implications and the fact that they form part of a much wider decision-making universe help to explain why the information policy-making process is still at a relatively early stage of development. Nevertheless, it is a developing process, with constituent elements and an operational framework evolving along broadly similar lines in many parts of the world.

Whereas the widespread popularity of the United Nations Information System in Science and Technology (UNISIST) model provides one example of the similarities in the policy-making process, further illustration can be derived from a comparison of this general approach with that adopted in specific policy studies. Hence a juxtaposition of Tocatlian's three conditions with those identified as essential in the Arthur D. Little study of information policy in the Netherlands reveals the fundamental coherence in approach, with the Little study giving specific expression to the common themes of identification, implementation and promotion, albeit in more elaborate form.[11] This juxtaposition is presented in Table 6, which, in addition to demonstrating the essential continuity of approach, can serve as a broad overview of the elements and framework of the information policy-making process.

Although the actual policy-making process is unlikely to be everywhere as orderly or as formalised as might be implied by the contents of Table 6, the elements listed in it are all important to policy development. Moreover, while the significance of information policy should by now be apparent, subsumed within the policy-making process are certain elements which, although perhaps less obvious in this context, are of critical importance to the general national well-being. For present purposes, two examples drawn from Table 6 should suffice to make the point. These comprise the wider implications of two of the elements identified by the Arthur D. Little study, that is the

Table 6. Key elements in the information policy-making process

Identification	Identification of the information requirements of society (Tocatlian).
	Identification of underlying purposes or goals for which policies should be designed (Little).
	Specification of general needs (Little).
Implementation	Devising means to ensure that the information requirements of society are met (Tocatlian).
	Identification of the strategic options available and the related resource requirements and constraints (Little).
	Selection of specific strategy options and of particular policies to support these options (Little).
Promotion	Development of awareness and understanding of the situation and of the issues involved (Little).
	Promotion of the effective use of information resources (Tocatlian).

identification of underlying purposes or goals and the specification of general needs. The first of these examples involves nothing less than that complex of goals and values that together go to make up the distinguishing characteristics of individual nations. In acknowledging the difficulty of specifying policy choices in such circumstances, the Little study nonetheless identified three assumptions as basic to underlying purpose so far as the Netherlands was concerned. These were the desirability of policy and other changes to enable the country to participate effectively in the global information marketplace; the need to protect national economic viability and growth potential; and the necessity of preserving national social and cultural values.[11] So far as general needs are concerned, these span a range of infrastructure and human capital requirements, notably in the fields of education and training, the telecommunications infrastructure and the regulatory environment of broadcasting and cable, the information industry, and public information provision.[11] It is on such grounds that claims for the centrality of information policy to the wider policy-making process are beginning to be heard.

Structures for policy making

Most countries operate some form of information policy, and the structures upon which these policies are based vary with local social and political conditions. Allowing for such variation and for the different levels of coordination involved, there is normally some locus or, indeed, loci for decision making, as the essence of any policy is planning. In the United Kingdom, where no one government department has overall responsibility for national information policy, there is considerable official involvement both designated and unstated. There is also a range of consultative machinery facilitating both inter-departmental liaison and an input both from information interests and from the wider community. The department most closely identified with national information policy is the Office of Arts and Libraries (OAL), although, as its name implies, the concern tends to be mainly with those aspects of policy related to the provision of library and information services. This fact is emphasised through its links with the Library and Information Services Council (LISC) and the British Library, which, as bodies which advise the Minister for the Arts on all aspects of library and information services, are clearly important components of the information policy-making structure.

The OAL plays an essentially facilitating and coordinating role in this process. It acts as a source of advice and assistance, as a body for liaison between the information policy activities of functional departments and their agencies, and as a promoter of approved policies and practices. Furthermore, working through the Library and Information Services Council for England (LISC Met.) and the rather more informally constituted bodies for Scotland, Wales and Northern Ireland, the OAL serves as a point of contact for both the providers and the users of information services. Moreover, when on occasion some form of direction is needed where an issue does not fall neatly within a defined departmental jurisdiction, the Minister for the Arts can raise the matter with the appropriate source.[12] Finally, linked through the everyday apparatus of committees and working parties to bodies such as the Library Association, the Institute of Information Scientists, and Aslib, the Association for Information Management, the OAL is a focal point in the national structure of the library and information policy-making process.

Despite the qualifications expressed as to the nature of such activities, however, involvement with the traditional information sector and, in particular, with the British Library Research and Development Department (BLR&DD), ensures that, in practice, the work of the OAL extends beyond what would be implied in its responsibility for library and information services. Since its inception in 1974, the BLR&DD has supported a wide variety of research activities in such fields as library automation; information technology; and information needs and provision in the life sciences, the social sciences and the humanities. It has also supported a number of important centres for research into fields as diverse as cataloguing and reprographics, primary communication and user studies.[9] Moreover, while on occasion this research included various policy issues, in 1985 the BLR&DD Advisory Council for Applied Research and Development (ACARD) recommended the creation of a new high-priority information policy programme, based upon previous research efforts in the spheres of information policy, library policy and economics of information.[9] This programme could lead to significant new departures not just in the work of the BLR&DD but in the field of information policy, where already links are being forged with the new Information and Communications Policy programme of the Economic and Social Research Council (ESRC). However, even if it lives up to the highest expectations of its creators, the British Library's information policy programme on its own is unlikely to meet national needs in this area. In any case, it constitutes only one element, albeit an important one, in the process of information policy making in the United Kingdom.

Many of these other elements are unstated – they are not commonly perceived as falling within an information policy context. Previous chapters have contained reference to the liberalisation of telecommunications in the United Kingdom, to the Alvey Programme on Advanced Information Technology, to the ITAP Report on tradeable information, to cable access television, to computer literacy, and, among other things, to the United Kingdom's response to the crisis over the Siberian gas pipeline. Whereas these and related matters involve questions of education and science, trade and technology, social welfare and international relations, they are all, in greater or lesser degree, part of the overall structure of information policy. The central principle underlying information policy is that of access to information. The structures which facilitate such access are by definition information policy structures even if, in the main, they go under the rubric of information technology policy, innovation policy, telecommunications policy or whatever. This fact in no way detracts from the credentials of such policies within their primary fields. It merely reflects the inexorable growth in the influence of information and its related technologies, to the point where decisions in just about every major field of activity today so often turn out to have implications for information policy. It also explains why there is no single, central authority, no tightly coordinated structure for information policy making in the United Kingdom, and, indeed, why the planning process in this field remains such a difficult proposition for most countries. Although more could be said on this question of structures, attention will now turn to the role of the major participants in the policy-making process. This adjustment of focus will in any case raise further structure-related issues, such as the role of government in the policy process and the extent to which a degree of centralisation may be considered necessary.

Participants in the information policy-making process

The process of information policy making involves, or should involve, a wide range of participants. Moreover, while crucial, the role of government, at least in the West, is dependent upon a variety of circumstances, not least the actions of other participants. Other participants include organisations in both the primary and secondary information sectors, public and private sector enterprises, academic and research interests, professional bodies and learned societies, user and public interest groups, the media, employers' organisations, and the trade unions. Although in ways an ideal listing, it is important to bear in mind the potential range of participants. Equally important is the need to distinguish between those players who have a recognised role in the policy process and those whose participation is much less apparent, but no less real for all that.

One of the major difficulties in the development and enhancement of the information policy process lies in the area of user involvement. The concept of a community of information users is one that seems to be infinitely expandable, to include on the one hand, specific groups of specialist users, and on the other, society as a whole. Somewhat ironically, it can also include non-users of information, because while non-use or underuse of available resources entails a direct diminution of direct user input to the policy process, the very fact of non-use provides a form of negative feedback to the policy makers.

Among the more direct channels for feedback from information users are the LISCs in the United Kingdom, and, in the United States, the National Commission on Libraries and Information Science (NCLIS). In addition to user involvement in their everyday work, both these organisations provide opportunities for direct public feedback through, respectively, the annual meeting of LISC with the library and information community, and the White House Conference on Libraries and Information Services. Again, across the spectrum of user communities, there is machinery for communication with those decision makers whose actions ultimately determine the shape and content of information policy. National libraries and academies of science and, in Britain, the Royal Society's Scientific Information Committee are obvious examples. There is also machinery for the users of such services as telecommunications and online information to make their views known to service providers and policy makers, both at national and international level.

However, where online users and similar groups are capable of making their views known in the appropriate policy-making circles, there is still a problem in regard to involvement of the public as a whole. Although this was a basic reason behind the creation of national sounding boards such as the LISCs, it is increasingly apparent that if the policy-making base is to be widened in this fashion, then a major educational effort is going to be required. As, in many cases, government itself has been slow to recognise the significance of the information resource, it is hardly surprising that large numbers of ordinary citizens should be ignorant of the situation. In the United Kingdom, there have been calls for the promotion of information awareness, alongside existing computer literacy and IT-awareness programmes.[13] While such an exercise would require the cooperation of various participants in the policy-making process, it is ultimately the responsibility of government.

Government and information policy

The role of government is critical to the success of the information policy process. However, while there is widespread recognition of the importance of the government contribution, there is also considerable difference of opinion over the nature and scale of state involvement. In effect, the form and substance of government involvement is reflected in the answers to two broad questions: whether or not the policy process should be centralised; and the extent, if any, to which government ought to intervene in the market for information goods and services.

Centralisation and the information policy process

The information industry has been a consistent critic of both centralisation and government intervention. As such it has done much to advance the cause of deregulation in the interests of open, more competitive markets. Nowhere has this been more in evidence than in the United States, the bastion of free enterprise and rugged individualism. Nevertheless, signs of movement in the American position suggest that it may not have been so uniform or clearcut as was previously thought. For example, an apparent anathema to government interference has to be balanced against the considerable boost given to both the information industry and information policy by large-scale government investments in research and development. It was in the post-Sputnik era that a number of leading information companies had their beginnings. However, it was during the 1970s that the Federal authorities began to give serious consideration to United States weaknesses in the information policy field. This can be explained by the actions of foreign governments and PTTs, which began to affect the overseas trading activities of American corporations.

In 1976, the Rockefeller Report called for the development of a national information policy that was sufficiently responsive to the new technologies and to the implications of the information age.[14] Three years later the Salmon Report set out information policy objectives in such areas as peace and security, trade and investment, free flow, equitable access to radiofrequencies and orbital slots, aid for development, and technological innovation.[14] Then in 1981 the Information Science and Technology Act, the Telecommunications Competition and Deregulation Act, and the International Communications Reorganisation Act were all passed. The purposes of the Telecommunications Competition and Deregulation Act are self-explanatory and some of its effects have been encountered in previous chapters. The Information Science and Technology Act created an Institute for Information Policy and Research, as an independent agency of the Federal Executive branch, and called for action on policy options and the planning and coordination of Federal research in areas related to information science and technology.[15] The International Communications Reorganisation Act established a Council on International Communications within the Executive Office of the President to coordinate all Federal information and communication policies.[15]

Although this legislation had more to do with unifying and coordinating information policy making than anything else, its enactment would suggest that in the past it was pragmatism rather than principle that underpinned American opposition to centralisation. In the United States, as elsewhere, the importance of proper planning for the information policy process has been realised, and with it the need for structures to support the diverse and at times conflicting activities of the organisations and individuals involved. In fact, developments in the United States are broadly in line with the thrust of the UNISIST recommendations as they refer to the development of a national information policy.[16] Although the process is by no means complete, the important thing is that the Federal Government has recognised its responsibilities in the area of national information policy. Moreover, what applies to the United States in this respect is equally applicable to the circumstances of other countries.

Government intervention in the marketplace

This question of government intervention in the market for information goods and services is fundamental to the development of national and international information policies, with implications far beyond the field of commerce. What is at issue is the nature and extent of government involvement, and not the principle of intervention itself. Government has always been involved in the information market, playing both a regulatory and a participatory role. However, with the emergence of entire information sectors in the advanced economies, the activities of government have come in for considerable scrutiny.

Although at one level such involvement is inevitable, there are also elements of chance and, indeed, default behind the fact of government participation in the information marketplace. When the information industry was in its infancy, governments and their agencies exercised certain regulatory and supervisory functions in respect of, for example, copyright, the telephone system or the mass media. With the transformation of market structures, the convergence of once disparate activities and technologies, and the appearance of an entirely new range of information goods and services, there was a corresponding, and largely accidental, transformation in the role and responsibilities of government. Moreover, when government intervention in the market has been necessary in the national interest, this has largely been by default, because no one else was willing to take the risk. This tends to occur on the basis of some or all of the following factors: public goods-type investment in, say, defence or basic health care; defence and other strategic considerations to do with national telecommunications and information systems; and the need to respond to the market behaviour of other governments or of foreign companies.[17] If these instances of involvement by accident or default comprised the sum total of government intervention in the marketplace, then the problems would be nowhere so acute. Unfortunately, the situation is rather more complicated than this.

In the first place, governments have always been major creators of information. Over the years, much of this information has been available either free of charge or at very nominal cost. However, government is no more immune to social and technological change than its counterparts in the private sector. Consequently, the development of an information industry and, in particular, the growth of trade in value-added information services have had considerable implications for the role of government in the marketplace. Of particular significance has been the opportunity to develop their supply side activities on a genuinely commercial basis.

In the second place, it is this potential change of role, or, strictly speaking, the possible enhancement of government activities on the supply side, that is the major area of contention. The basis for opposition to the idea of increased government involvement in the supply of information goods and services is that by its presence government distorts the free market and confronts other suppliers with unfair competition. It is certainly the case that, subsidised as they are from public funds, and immune to the more drastic penalties for business failure, government enterprises enjoy several significant advantages over those in the private sector. Indeed, the very fact that an information product bears the government trademark could well enhance its attractiveness to potential customers.[18] On the other hand, by being forced to rely on the public sector, government departments can face delays, inefficiencies and increased costs, all of which at some point begin to have an adverse effect upon services to the public.[19]

An important consideration in information policy formulation is the matter of public access to government information. This is as relevant to the 'freedom of information' issue as it is to the development of value-added services built upon the packaging and resale of publicly available government information. Some would argue that all such information should be available free of charge, or at nominal cost, simply because of the public investment involved in its production. Others would deplore the disposal of such valuable public property at noncommercial rates, especially to enterpreneurs themselves seeking to make a profit from its resale. As to the best means of exploiting this national resource, it can be argued that where governments can offer a service at a lower price than private sector companies it is in the public interest for them to do so. Apart from considerations of unfair competition and the possibly adverse effects upon individual innovation and initiative, such a development, if pursued to any great extent, would represent a major change in the policy of most governments. In any case, a more likely scenario in such circumstances would be some form of liberalisation or deregulation, probably as the forerunner for 'privatisation' and the sale of the organisation on the open market.

Such debatable considerations aside, however, there is a fair measure of agreement on the role of government in the information market. Indeed, in many respects this consensus extends across the spectrum of information policy, with opinion on one issue reinforcing that on another. The consensus tends to be that government should play an essentially supportive role in the marketplace, one that stimulates competition and helps to create conditions for profitability and growth. In more specific terms, there is agreement on the need for infrastructure development in such areas as telecommunications, education and training, and research and development; as well as action in such areas as legislation, standardisation and consultation at the international level.[20] Likewise there is strong support for the widest possible dissemination of information held or created by government, with due regard for considerations of national security and personal privacy. There would also be well-nigh unanimous agreement on the importance of government support for the information industry, both directly through incentives and awareness programmes, and indirectly by exploiting its potential contribution to the modernisation and development of other industries. Many within the information industry would see this as an offshoot of the wider issue of private versus public provision, a matter which is discussed later. As regards direct assistance to the information industry, however, three potential government contributions have been identified: encouraging greater use of existing services by national and international organisations, developing legal and financial structures sympathetic to the industry and to its development, and initiating action on the removal of barriers and restrictions on trade.[20]

As regards the involvement of government in the information industry, therefore, opinion in the industry itself seems to favour a supporting and facilitating role, with direct market involvement confined to the demand side. By the same token, the consensus of opinion would be against any serious attempt by government to expand its role on the supply side, which is viewed largely as the province of the private sector. Given a major change in the political climate, however, attitudes towards the information industry and its operational environment could change.

National information policies

Allowing for differences in terminology as well as in social and political systems, all governments today operate some form of national information policy. The two major stimuli to the development of these policies have been the need to respond to advances in the new technologies and to the accompanying political and economic changes. For developing countries, this has meant little more than an addition to, or a reformulation of, their existing problems of underdevelopment and dependency. For the more advanced nations, it has brought new urgency to the need for competitiveness in international markets and, paradoxically, a kind of vulnerability through strength. As has been seen above, this explains why the United States has found it necessary to devise a national policy in defence of its increasingly embattled global information interests. This section will concentrate upon information policy developments in a small number of economically advanced countries: the United States, Japan, France, and the United Kingdom. It will also give brief consideration to the information activities of the United Nations and some of its agencies, and to the information market policy of the EEC.

The United States

In many respects the United States is a microcosm of all the problems inherent in trying to formulate a coherent information policy in an open and democratic society. There are myriad interests to be taken into account, both public and private, and, in addition to actual policies, a vast range of regulations and practices. Nor do such considerations exist in a vacuum, because, as well as tackling domestic information issues, there is the need to harmonise the resulting policies with those on international trade, aid and foreign affairs.[21] As a result several trends in the development of information policy in the United States can be identified.

First has been a noticeable widening in the scope of such policies, from an original concern with scientific and technical information towards policies geared to the development and exploitation of information as a national resource.[22] Second has been a trend towards policies designed to strengthen the workings of the free market, by encouraging competition and removing actual or potential barriers to internal trade in information services. A key element here has been deregulation of the telecommunications system, to facilitate widespread access to highly efficient, low-cost communications, and to support interactive, high-value, network-based information and enter- tainment services.[23] Third has been a series of measures to ensure the maintenance of balance between the free flow of information, with all that this means for dissemination and access, and the protection of individual and communal rights in respect of privacy, security and moral standards. Lastly, there is the fundamental underlying trend towards an increased level of involvement by the Federal Government in the information policy arena.

The most obvious result of such developments is that the United States is now much better prepared for the policy challenges of the information age. As recently as 1980, the House Committee on Government Operations found that the United States lacked even the organisational structures to develop policies, coordinate actions and effectively protect its interests.[24] This provided the spur to establishment of the Council on International Communications and Information in 1981.[25] Its brief was to coordinate the development and implementation of a uniform, consistent and comprehensive United States policy in response to the problems raised by barriers to international information and communications flow. This Council is expected to have a limited lifespan, on the assumption that the real solutions to the problems of information policy will emerge within those government departments and agencies charged with specific responsibilities in the field. However, a membership which includes, in addition to an independent director, the Secretaries of State and Commerce, the Chairman of the Federal Communications Commission, the United States Trade Representative, the Director of the Office of Management and Budget, and the Assistant to the President for National Security Affairs should leave in no doubt the importance of national information policy.[25]

Japan

In Japan, information policy has a long and impressive history. While many Western observers would attribute the current success of Japanese industry to advances made in the period of reconstruction following the Second World War, the process of Japanese modernisation in fact dates back to the time of the Meiji Restoration in 1868. Fired with enthusiasm for economic development, the Japanese embarked on a quest for knowledge and information which is still continuing today. It seems clear that Japan came to understand the value and significance of information much earlier than any of her competitors, one result of which was the development of policies designed to harness and exploit it. More than a century after the Meijis came to power, it was still noticeable that, while in Europe and the United States information was seen as having no material value in itself, in Japan it was regarded as a kind of raw material, a factor basic to industrial competitiveness.[26]

Utilisation of this raw material through the process known as 'informatisation' has already been mentioned, as indeed have similar trends elsewhere. In Japan, however, the informatisation process is much more institutionalised. Thus, the so-called 'visions', which for so long have provided the basis for much of Japanese public policy, are the product of detailed discussions at Councils whose membership is truly representative of every stratum of society.[27] Although other countries have their own machinery for public consultation, the sheer scale of such activities in Japan, and their integration with the general social system, both help to explain the success of subsequent policy and emphasise the strength of its social orientation.

The overall goal to which such policies are geared is that of a stable society with an 'oil free' economic structure by the twenty-first century. The basic elements of Japanese information policy are fourfold: increased human welfare, international cooperation through information use, development of pioneer technology, and development of Japanese information resources.[27] Although the first two of these policy elements may be self-explanatory, a word or two about each of the others might not go amiss. First, while the pioneer technologies include opto-electronics, Josephson Junctions, bionics and mechatronics, the ultimate objective of this research activity is not technological superiority but freedom from dependence on natural energy resources.[27] Second, the drive to develop Japanese information resources is aimed not at the enhancement of local sources and provision but at redressing the currently adverse balance of trade in information.[27]

The basis for current policies emerged in the 1960s as Japan sought to restructure an economy heavily committed to declining heavy industries and very dependent upon exports. A solution to the problem was found in the new technologies, both as a source of exports and as the basis for modernising Japanese industry and society. As a result of the successful implementation of these policies, Japan has become a symbol of efficiency and quality, not just in fields such as motor cars and consumer electronics, but also in VLSI, space technology, communications, energy research, chemical and biological engineering, and mechatronics. The policies which produced these results are still in operation today, and involve the offer of subsidies for research and development in the new technologies, selective protectionism for new ventures, government procurement initiatives, and low-cost loans to approved developments.[28] For those countries which can follow this example, there is the prospect of growth, employment and prosperity. For those who cannot, especially those which lack energy resources or alternative sources of wealth creation, the future could be bleak indeed. So far as the Japanese are concerned, if their latest initiatives enjoy anything like the success of these earlier policies, then the stated goal of world information leadership must be a very real possibility.[29]

France

Although the scale of the problem of matching the Japanese challenge is beyond the resources of any single European country, France has made its intentions in the matter very clear. Like the Japanese, the French were quick to appreciate the resource characteristics of information. Indeed, it was a Frenchman, Louis Joinet, who in 1977 coined the now-familiar phrase about information being power and economic information being economic power.[29] Like the Japanese, moreover, the French reviewed a range of future economic and social scenarios, placing a special emphasis on the need to find new sources of technological development and economic growth. The best-known and most comprehensive of such studies was the Nora–Minc report. Although its original concern was with what the French termed 'telematique' – the convergence of telecommunications and data processing technologies – the Nora–Minc report came to form the basis for information policy in France. Outlining both specific functions and structures for what was in effect a national informatics plan, it addressed questions of social change as well as of technological and industrial development. In addition to setting out the roles and responsibilities of central government and its relevant agencies and departments, it provided for a cabinet-level post to ensure the coordination and effective implementation of information policy.[30]

The broad thrust of this policy involves action in the areas of new information products and services, in the infrastructure, and in user education. There is also provision for certain measures to protect the national interest, both by means of selective tariff and nontariff barriers and, as mentioned in a previous chapter, by taxing transborder dataflows. Owing to the convergence not just of technologies but of functions based upon them it can be difficult to separate, say, infrastructure activities from those in the information services industry. Thus, in addition to PTT involvement in such fields as fibre optics and two-way information systems, it has also been charged with the goal of providing an interactive terminal and, eventually, a facsimile device in all homes equipped with a telephone. This has already enhanced national capabilities in the manufacture of telecommunications hardware and its associated software.[30] Moreover, in the field of information services many firms and institutions are engaged in the creation of online services and of databases and databanks. To this end they have received considerable assistance from government, which has provided not just funds but also effective support facilities through such agencies as Mission Interministerielle d'Information Scientifique et Technique (MIDIST) and Agence de l'Informatique (ADI).[30]

In the field of human capital development, on the other hand, a number of measures have been taken to accelerate the development of IT awareness among the community as a whole. In 1980, the Government announced plans for the eventual introduction of 10,000 microcomputers into schools, including provision for training up to an additional 1,000 teachers a year to teach children how to use this equipment.[30] Also, considerable emphasis is being placed on making the man or woman in the street more aware of the existence of information goods and services. Of particular interest, however, are attempts to make people aware of the value of information itself, whether as users or producers of the commodity. Within the country's engineering schools, staff and students are being encouraged not only to use online systems but also to contribute directly to the improvement of services by involving themselves in the production and marketing of databases.[31] As with the Japanese example, the careful review and analysis of needs and opportunities, the judicious involvement of government, and an emphasis on the wider social dimension are all part of the information policy process in France.

The United Kingdom

Each of these elements is also present to varying degree in the information policy process in the United Kingdom. As elsewhere, moreover, this is a many-sided business, with, consequently, an urgent need for coordination both of the process and of the policies which emerge from it. Furthermore, as in all such situations, certain priorities come to the fore, with such contributions as the OAL's documents on the Future Development of Library and Information Services (FDLIS) attracting much less attention than those linked more directly to output, growth and employment. Indeed, the central cohesive element in United Kingdom information policy is probably action in the field of information technology. Current developments in this sphere can be traced back to the recommendations of ACARD, first in 1978 with regard to semi-conductor technology, and then in 1980 with proposals for the appointment of a Minister for Information Technology.[32]

The acceptance and implementation of these ACARD recommendations and the appointment of an Information Technology Minister within the DTI were an indication of the importance attached to such matters by successive United Kingdom governments. The Minister's brief is extensive and includes the coordination and promotion of IT policies and assistance in creating the necessary framework and conditions for development. The principal means of implementation have been through the funding of a wide range of application and awareness programmes, through support for research and development, through initiatives in the fields of education and training, and by means of legislative and regulatory activity.[33] Prominent among such developments have been programmes designed to foster the spread of microelectronics in industry, as well as the Micros in Primary Schools Programme and the Microelectronics Education Programme (MEP). The diversity of such initiatives and the pervasive influence of information technology in society mean that IT policy and information policy are closely related. Indeed, they frequently turn out to be one and the same thing. From the wide range of initiatives emerging from these policies, three have been chosen to indicate the nature and scale of the British approach: the MEP, the IT '82 Project and the Alvey Programme.

The MEP was introduced in 1981 and funded to the extent of £9 million for a five-year period. Financed by the Department of Education and Science (DES) and administered by the Council for Educational Technology (CET), its major objectives were to help prepare children for life in a technological society and to assist teachers in the use of information technology. The major thrust of this very successful project was threefold: the development of software and teaching materials, pilot courses for in-service teacher training, and a network of 14 regional centres to coordinate the production and distribution of information.[33] IT '82 aimed at a different and much wider audience. Its objective was to promote greater knowledge and awareness of the opportunities and benefits of IT among the community at large, through the nomination of 1982 as Information Technology Year in the United Kingdom. The campaign was coordinated by the DTI, which provided almost £2.5 million for the purpose, to which private industry added nearly £2 million more, largely in kind rather than in cash. Included in the programme were mobile exhibition units, publicity campaigns in the national media, and video productions. It was estimated that over one million people heard a series of special radio broadcasts during 1982. It was further estimated that, whereas only one person in six of the population had heard about IT at the start of the campaign, this figure had reached a level of more than three in five by its conclusion.[33]

The Alvey Programme on Advanced Information Technology is the major United Kingdom response to the Japanese challenge. The result of proposals emanating from a committee chaired by John Alvey, the programme involves collaborative research between industry and academic institutions, with a budget of £350 million for a five-year period that began in 1983. The financial sponsors are the DES, the DTI and the Ministry of Defence. The programme covers research and development activity in four basic areas: very large-scale integration, software engineering, expert systems and intelligent knowledge-based systems, and man–machine interface. Oversight of the programme is the responsibility of a small Directorate assisted by specialist committees.[34] There can be little disputing the importance of the Alvey Programme, whether as an attempt to do something about the highly fragmented nature of the United Kingdom research community or because of its focus on the enabling technologies. It has attracted more than its share of criticism, largely on the grounds that the funding provided is insufficient for the task. Certainly it is not over-endowed with cash, and although Alvey originally sought 100 per cent funding for each project, the Government insisted that only academic institutions would qualify for this level of support, with companies receiving 50 per cent of research costs. In effect, this has meant that small firms, who have been responsible for a great deal of innovation in the information industry, have lost out heavily in this respect to the big companies.[35]

Apart from anything else, this seems to be rather at odds with stated Government policies of encouragement to individual enterprise and initiative through the promotion of competition.[36] However, while Alvey may be a case of too little, it is by no means certain that it has come too late. In any case, Alvey was always intended to complement the European Community's ESPRIT programme, itself recognition of the fact that no single European country could compete with the Americans and the Japanese on its own. Indeed, the presence of such realities is powerful support for those arguments in favour of coherent, well-planned national and international information policies. For the moment, attention is focussed on the United Kingdom Government's immediate intentions as the Alvey Programme nears the end of its five-year term.

A cautionary note

Having drawn notice to the similarities in approaches to national information policy, it is also necessary to point out that there are distinct differences in the ways in which individual countries plan and implement these policies. In France, for example, rather more attention is paid to detailed planning and preparation than in the United Kingdom. Again, while there have been high social costs to the Japanese economic miracle, there nevertheless seems to be a greater awareness of the social dimension to information policy in Japan than in either the United Kingdom or the United States. Furthermore, while neither could be accused of ignoring the human dimension, differences in the respective political systems in the United Kingdom and the United States are reflected in information policy, notably in the role of government. Nonetheless, more than any other European country, the United Kingdom has followed the American lead in freeing the market for information goods and services. In noting both differences and similarities, however, the question remains as to the extent to which policies devised for application in one country can succeed in the different social, economic, political and cultural circumstances of another. This is a question of particular relevance for those organisations whose responsibilities for information policy are international rather than national in scope.

International organisations

International information policies emerge from basically the same matrix as national information policies. Although the correlation is not always exact, the overlap between the domestic and external interests of nations produces a close relationship between national and international information policies. As will by now be obvious, there is scarcely a major international organisation that is not in some way involved in the business of information policy. Examples include the United Nations and its agencies, the International Telecommunications Union (ITU), the International Telecommunications Users Group (INTUG), the ISO, and the OECD. In the space which remains, brief mention will be made of the information policy activities of three organisations: Unesco, the Intergovernmental Bureau of Informatics and the EEC.

Unesco

Unesco's formal involvement in information policy dates from 1966 and the launch of a project to test the feasibility of a world science information system. With objectives that included assistance with infrastructure improvements, as well as the development and enhancement of information systems, this UNISIST programme was followed by another, more general, project in 1974, the National Information Systems Programme (NATIS). NATIS was based on the premise that governments have a responsibility to ensure maximum public access to information resources and that this is best discharged through the formulation of information policies for incorporation into national development plans. As with the UNISIST programme, Unesco provides assistance to member states for the planning and development of national policies.[37] In 1976, both these programmes were merged to form the PGI. The overall framework for Unesco's information activities has four sectors: promotion of policies and plans, promotion of methods and norms, promotion of infrastructure development and modern techniques, and promotion of the education and training of both information specialists and information users.[37]

The Intergovernmental Bureau of Informatics (IBI)

The IBI has emerged as a staunch defender of the interests of the developing world and as a force in international information circles. Founded by Unesco in 1961 as the International Computation Centre, it was re-organised on an independent basis as the IBI in 1974. More than a change of title, this mirrored global developments in information and its related technologies, and the emergence of informatics. Through a variety of dissemination and assistance programmes, the IBI helps developing nations to respond to the challenges of a world where informatics is part of 'realpolitik'. Its First World Conference on Strategies and Policies for Informatics (SPIN), held jointly with Unesco at Torremolinos, Spain in 1978, set the seal on its avowedly political interpretation of informatics. Two subsequent conferences on transborder dataflow in 1980 and 1984, and the so-called 'Declaration of Mexico' on informatics, development and peace issued in 1981, are further developments of this policy. The IBI is striving to change the present situation of dependency which obtains between the developed and the developing worlds by effecting a new division of technological and other resources through the medium of informatics.[38]

The EEC

The EEC is a major user and creator of all kinds of information. Whereas most of the Community's 20 Directorates-General, or DGs, would have interest in some area of information policy, this interest is particularly marked in the case of six of them. These are DG-III, Internal Market and Industrial Affairs; DG-IV, Competition; DG-V, Employment, Social Affairs and Education; DG-XII, Science, Research and Development; DG-XIII, Telecommunications, Information Industry and Innovation; and DG-XVI, Regional Policy. The Committee on Information and Documentation in Science and Technology (CIDST) plays an important role in the formulation of Community information policy, two of whose major elements, the Community Information Market Policy and ESPRIT, have already been mentioned in previous chapters.

It should suffice at this point to reiterate that the Information Market Policy is an attempt to create the conditions for a viable European information market, capable of withstanding Japanese and American competition. The intention is to utilise existing national structures and facilities, with action taken to harmonise different frameworks, remove internal trade barriers, and facilitate the movement of labour and capital throughout the Community. A similar approach underlies the ESPRIT programme of collaborative, pre-competitive research and development in information technology.[39]

Information policy: the future

It would be difficult to overstate the importance of information policy to the aspirations and plans of individual nations, and to the future of world trade and international relations. However, while some specific issues have been identified here, it is unlikely that the piecemeal resolution of individual problems will do much to change the totality of the international information environment. Indeed, Giuliano has described such concerns as sovereignty and privacy as 'symptom issues', and as such not to be confused with the fundamentals of information policy. These he adjudges to be in such areas as education and training, the legal system, and the apparatus of government regulation.[40] In making this point, Giuliano, in essence, is drawing attention to the fact that, whether at national or international level, information policy is ultimately a matter for government. It is a political question.

In fact, all those arguments over 'free or fee', the public or private provision of information, or free flow versus control are, at heart, arguments about the extent, rather than the principle, of government involvement. In the absence of government funding for research and development, and for official publication and dissemination programmes, there would be serious question marks over the viability of large sections of the information industry. Nor is there any evident difference in principle between the informatics policies of developing nations and the support given to multinational corporations by governments in the advanced countries, especially when these information policies have very often evolved as a form of defence against the market behaviour of the multinationals. In such circumstances, moreover, the free flow of information can often turn out to be a euphemism for the abuse of market power and the continued exploitation of weaker trading partners.

Not that all the blame for the unsettled state of international information relations is to be laid at the door of the major information powers. Freedom of information laws in the United States can operate to the disadvantage of American organisations by resulting in the loss of valuable information to overseas rivals, who can simply access the information through online databases. Likewise, material which is protected by United States copyright legislation can simply be pirated in countries which recognise no such constraints. Finally, many of the benefits accruing from deregulation of the United States telecommunications system can be eroded at the point of interconnection with heavily regulated or state-controlled networks elsewhere, where tariffs may be higher and the range of services more restricted.[40] There remains an urgent need for international reciprocity, and for a measure of consensus on the deeper issues which underlie both national information policies and the relations between nations.

If such progress is to be achieved it will not happen overnight, nor on the basis of such radical attempts to change the pattern of international relations as the NWICO. Less confrontational methods are called for, especially in view of the urgent need for international agreement on the vexed question of trade in services. At present, trade in services is not covered by the GATT, and while the West would like to see this happen, it would be unpopular in the developing world, because of its massive trade deficits in this area. On such a basis have emerged the informatics policies of countries such as Brazil, India and Mexico. These developments testify to the inseparability of trade and politics, and to the influence of the critical linking factor, which is information. The policies being devised to exploit this information factor are among the strongest indicators that, underlying these sociopolitical issues, is an event of even more fundamental significance. Although still in its infancy and uneven in its distribution, this event is the emergence of the information society.

References

1. Rosenberg, Victor, National information policies, in *Annual review of information science & technology*, ed. M. E. Williams, vol. 17, White Plains, New York, 1982, 3–32.
2. Rubin, Michael, Rogers, ed., *Information economics and policy in the United States*, Littleton, Colorado, Libraries Unlimited, 1983, 8.
3. Bushkin, Arthur and Jane H. Yurow, *The foundations of United States information policy: a U.S. government submission to the high-level conference on information, computer and communications policy*, OECD, 6–8 October 1980, Paris, Washington, DC, US Department of Commerce, 1980. (NTIA-SP-80-8.)
4. Kawahata, M., Significance of informationalization and the basic lines of informationalization policy, in *Information policy and scientific research*, ed. Arie N. Manten and Theo Tinman, Amsterdam, Elsevier, 1983, 35–37.
5. Brown, Royston, Towards a national information policy, *Aslib Proceedings*, 34, 6/7, June/July 1982, 317–24.
6. Bushkin and Yurow, op. cit., 4.
7. *The Netherlands in the information age: a context for discussion on information policy in the Netherlands*, Cambridge, Massachusetts, Arthur D. Little, 1981.
8. Manten and Tinman, op. cit., 10–12.
9. British Library Research and Development Department, 'Information Policy Research'. Report of a meeting held at the Castle Hotel, Windsor, 7–8 July 1985. Unpublished.
10. Tocatlian, Jacques, 'National information and the General Information

Programme/UNISIST'. Paper presented at a symposium, Vienna, 5–6 April 1984.

11. *The Netherlands in the information age*, op. cit., 132–34.

12. Brown, op. cit., 319.

13. Anthony, L. J., National information policy, *Aslib Proceedings*, 34, 6/7, June/July 1982, 310–16.

14. Rosenberg, op. cit., 6.

15. Chartrand, R. J., Government's role in the information society, *Journal of Information Science, Principles and Practice*, 5, 1982–83, 137–42.

16. Unesco, *First UNISIST meeting of experts on regional information policy and planning for economic and social development: a dynamic approach*. Working document prepared by Mr John C. Gray, Paris, Unesco, 1977.

17. Hirst, W. N., Towards a national information policy: some observations from a science and technology perspective. Paper presented at the National Information Policy Seminar organised by the Library Association of Australia, ACT Branch, Canberra, 7–8 December 1981.

18. Rubin, op. cit., 79.

19. Horton, Forest W., Jr, *Understanding U.S. information policy: the information policy primer*, Washington, DC, Information Industry Association, 1982, 37.

20. Anthony, op. cit., 311.

21. Horton, op. cit., 44.

22. Berninger, Douglas E. and Burton W. Atkinson, Interaction between the public and private sectors in national information policies, in *Annual review of information science & technology*, ed. M.E. Williams, vol. 13, White Plains, New York, Knowledge Industry Publications, 1978, 3–36.

23. *The Netherlands in the information age*, op. cit., 136.

24. Eger, John, The global phenomenon of teleinformatics: an introduction, *Cornell International Law Journal*, 14, 1981, 203–36.

25. Berninger and Atkinson, op. cit., 3–36.

26. Galinski, Christian, Information: the basis of Japan's forecast technological development, *Aslib Proceedings*, 36, 1, January 1984, 24–57.

27. Kawahata, op. cit., 39.

28. Rubin, op. cit., 319.

29. Eger, op. cit., 319.

30. Michel, Jean, Information now: a French point of view, in Manten and Tinman, op. cit., 129–32.

31. Ibid., 131.

32. Rubin, op. cit., 320.

33. McLaughlin, Robert and Anthony Foley, *Information technology in Northern Ireland and the Republic of Ireland*, Belfast, Cooperation North, 1985, 40.

34. Alvey Directorate, *Progress report*, July 1983.

35. Lloyd, J., To have and have not, *New Scientist*, 105, 1442, 7 February 1985, 37–38.

36. Stewart, J. Allen, The government's role, *Aslib Proceedings*, 36, 1, January 1984, 1–6.

37. Taylor, L. J., comp., *A librarian's handbook*, vol. 2, London, Library Association, 1980.

38. Intergovernmental Bureau of Informatics, *IBI, informatics and the concert of nations*, Rome, IBI, 1985, 14–15.
39. McLaughlin and Foley, op. cit., 12.
40. Giuliano, V. E., The United States of America in the information age, in Manten and Tinman, op. cit., 59–76.

Bibliography

1. Adelstein, A.S., John E. Boules and Sheldon M. Harsel, *Information societies: comparing the Japanese and American experiences*, Seattle, International Communications Centre, 1978, 297 pp.

2. Alvey Committee, *A Programme for advanced information technology*, London, HMSO, 1982, 71 pp.

3. Alvey Directorate, *Progress report*, London, July 1983, 9 pp.

4. Anderla, Georges, The international data market revisited. Paper presented to Special Session of the Committee for Information, Computer and Communications Policy, Paris, OECD, 1983, 43 pp. Unpublished.

5. Anthony, L.J., National information policy, *Aslib Proceedings*, 34, 6/7, June/July 1982, 310–16.

6. Arrow, Kenneth J., The economics of information, in Dertouzous and Moses (see no. 37), 306–17.

7. Belkin, N.J., Information concepts for information science, *Journal of Documentation*, 34, 1, March 1978, 55–85.

8. Bell, Daniel, the information society, in Dertouzous and Moses (see no. 37), 163–211.

9. Berninger, Douglas C. and Burton W. Adkinson, Interaction between the public and private sectors in national information programs, in *Annual review of information science & technology*, ed. M. E. Williams, vol. 13, White Plains, New York, Knowledge Industry Publications, 1978, 3–36.

10. Blankenhorn, Dana, Waiting for ISDN, *Datamation*, International Edition, 1, July 1986, 83–88.

11. Bortnik, Jane, International information flow: the developing world perspective, *Cornell International Law Journal*, 14, 1981, 333–53.

12. Brake, Terence, *The need to know: teaching the importance of information*, London, British Library, 1980, 74 pp.

13. Brimmer, Carl W., U.S. telecommunications common carrier policy, in *Annual review of information science & technology*, ed. M. E. Williams, vol. 17, White Plains, New York, Knowledge Industry Publications, 1982, 33–82.

159

14. Brinberg, H.R., Information in the United States: an industry serving industry, in *Information and the transformation of society*, ed. G. P. Sweeney, Amsterdam, North Holland, 1982, 265–86.

15. Broadbent, Marianne, Information management and educational pluralism, *Education for Information*, 2, 1984, 209–27.

16. Brown, Royston, Towards a national information policy, *Aslib Proceedings*, 34, 6/7, June/July 1982, 317–24.

17. Buckland, Michael K., *Library services in theory and context*, London, Pergamon Press, 1983, 250 pp.

18. Burgess, B.C., ISDN and the digital future: user requirements in the marketplace. Paper presented at the Annual Conference of the Pacific Telecommunications Council, 15 January 1985, 9 pp. Unpublished.

19. Burgess, B.C., Restrictions on the transfer and use of international information. Paper presented at the ITU/American Bar Association World Forum, San Francisco, 1981, 15 pp. Unpublished.

20. Bushkin, Arthur A., The uses of technology: the new battleground in world trade. Paper presented at the Annual Institute on World Affairs, Ames, Iowa, 1983, 10 pp. Unpublished.

21. Bushkin, Arthur A. and Jane H. Yurow, *The foundations of U.S. information policy: a U.S. government submission to the high-level conference on information, computer and communications policy*, Paris, October 1980, Washington, DC, US Department of Commerce, 1980, 20 pp. (NTIA-SP-80-8.)

22. Business International, *Survey of the European Information Industry: its electronic developments*, Geneva, Business International, 1984, 179 pp.

23. Canadian Department of Communication, Consultative Committee on the implications of telecommunications for Canadian sovereignty, 1979. (The Clyne Report.)

24. Canisius, P., Information policies in Western Europe, *Aslib Proceedings*, 34, 1, January 1982, 13–24.

25. Cawkell, Anthony E., *Handbook of information technology and office systems*, Amsterdam, North Holland, 1986, 996 pp.

26. Cawkell, Anthony E., Information technology and communications, in *Annual review of information science & technology*, ed. M. E. Williams, vol. 15, White Plains, New York, Knowledge Industry Publications, 1980, 37–65.

27. Cherry, Colin, *On human communication: a review, a survey and a criticism*, New York, Wiley, 1957, 333 pp.

28. Chartrand, R.J., Government's role in the information society, *Journal of Information Science, Principles and Practice*, 5, 1982–83, 137–42.

29. Clifton, H.D., *Business data systems*, 3rd edn, Englewood Cliffs, New Jersey, Prentice Hall, 1986, 380 pp.

30. Commission of the European Communities, *Discussion paper on a Community information market policy*, Brussels, European Commission, 1985, 49 pp.

31. Commission of the European Communities, *European society faced with the challenge of the new information technologies*, Luxembourg, European Commission, 1979. (The Dublin Report.)

32. Craig, Lynn, *This is IT in education*, London, Channel 4 Television, 1984, 15 pp.

33. Crawford, Susan, The origin and development of a concept, the information society, *Bulletin of the Medical Library Association*, 71, 4, October 1983, 380–85.

34. Cronin, Blaise, The information society, *Aslib Proceedings*, 38, 4, April 1986, 121–29.

35. Cullen, John, Impact of information technology on human wellbeing, in *Information technology: impact on the way of life* (see no. 78), vol. 2.

36. Denicoff, Marvin, Sophisticated software: the road to science and Utopia, in Dertouzous and Moses (see no. 37), 367–91.

37. Dertouzous, Michael L. and Joel Moses, eds., *The computer age: a twenty year view*, Cambridge, Massachusetts, MIT Press, 1974, 491 pp.

38. Desoulier, N., Are we ready for an information policy?, in Manten and Tinman (see no. 95), 103–6.

39. Dizard, Wilson P., The coming information age, *The Information Society Journal*, 1, 2, 1981, 91–112.

40. Dordick, Herbert, Information society indicators: description, measurement, prediction, in Adelstein et al. (see no. 1).

41. East, Harry, Nonprofit organisations in the U.K. online database market, *Aslib Proceedings*, 38, 9, September 1986, 327–34.

42. Falk, Howard, Hardware corner: optical disk storage, *The Electronic Library*, 4, 12, 1980, 20–23.

43. Eger, John, The global phenomenon of teleinformatics: an introduction, *Cornell International Law Journal*, 14, 1981, 203–36.

44. Faibisoff, Sylvia and Donald P. Ely, Information and information systems, in *Key papers in the design and evaluation of information systems*, ed. D. W. King, White Plains, New York, Knowledge Industry Publications, 1978, 270–81.

45. Fairthorne, R.A., The theory of communication, *Aslib Proceedings*, 6, 4, November 1954, 255–67.

46. Farradane, J., The nature of information, *Journal of Information Science*, 1, 1979, 13–17.

47. Feketekuty, Geza and Jonathon David Aronson, Restrictions on trade in communications and information services, *The Information Society Journal*, 2, 3/4, 1984, 217–33.

48. Feketekuty, Geza and Kathryn Hauser, The impact of information technology on trade in services, 1985, 29 pp. Unpublished.

49. Flowerdew, A.D.J., C.M. Oldman and C.M.E. Whitehead, *The pricing and provision of information*, London, British Library, 1984, 92 pp. (British Library R&D Report 20).

50. Forester, Tom, ed., *The information technology revolution*, Oxford, Blackwell, 1985, 675 pp.

51. Fritz, R., The correlation of information and research policy, in Manten and Tinman (see no. 95), 107–11.

52. Fyson, Nance Lui, *The development puzzle*, 7th edn, London, Hodder & Stoughton, 1984, 189 pp.

53. Galinski, Christian, Information: the basis of Japan's forecast technological and economic development, *Aslib Proceedings*, 36, 1, January, 1984, 24–57.

54. Garfield, Eugene, Everyday problems in an information society, in Cawkell, *Handbook* (see no. 25), 883–88.

55. Garnham, Nicholas, The information society is also a class society, in *Information technology: impact on the way of life* (see no. 78).

56. Gleave, David, C. Angell and K. Woolley, *The impact of new technology on the labour market and demands for information services*, London, British Library, 1986, 330 pp.

57. Goldstein, Charles M., Computer-based information storage technologies, in *Annual review of information science & technology*, ed. M. E. Williams, vol. 19, White Plains, New York, Knowledge Industry Publications, 1984, 65–96.

58. Gosling, William, Information technology's seven league boots, *Political Quarterly*, 54, 1983, 120–26.

59. Gray, John C. and Brian Perry, *Scientific information*, London, OUP, 1975, 62 pp.

60. Great Britain, Department of Trade and Industry, *Information technology: the age of electronic information*, London, HMSO, 1982, 16.

61. Great Britain, Department of Trade and Industry, *Government response to the ITAP report on 'Making a business of information'*, London, HMSO, 1984, 53.

62. Grewlich, Klaus and Finn Pedersen, eds., *Power and participation in an information society*, Luxembourg, Commission of the European Communities, 1984, 289 pp.

63. Giuliano, V.E., The United States of America in the information age, in Manten and Tinman (see no. 95), 59–76.

64. Gupta, Amar, New developments and applications of microcomputer hardware and software, in Cawkell, *Handbook* (see no. 25).

65. Hamelink, Cees, ed., *Communication in the eighties: a reader on the Macbride Report*, Rome, IDOC International, 1980, 185 pp.

66. Harbury, Colin, *Economic behaviour: an introduction*, London, Allen & Unwin, 1980, 265 pp.

67. Harris, C. C., *Fundamental concepts and the sociological enterprise*, London, Croom Helm, 1980, 248 pp.

68. Harris, L. and E. Davis, System X and the evolving U.K. telecommunications network, *The Post Office Engineers Journal*, 72, 2, 1979, 7–13.

69. Hawkridge, David, Progress in educational information technology, in Cawkell, *Handbook* (see no. 25), 889–907.

70. Hayes, R., Information science in librarianship, *Libri*, 19, 3, 1969, 216–36.

71. Hayman, Caroline, The impact of telecommunications on education, *Political Quarterly*, 54, 1983, 152–59.

72. Hirst, W.N., Towards a national information policy: some observations from a science and technology perspective, in Library Association of Australia (see no. 87), 7–20.

73. Horton, Forest W., Jr, *Information resources management: concept and cases*, Cleveland, Ohio, Association for Systems Management, 1979, 343 pp.

74. Horton, Forest W., Jr, *Understanding U.S. information policy: the information policy primer*, Washington, DC, Information Industry Association, 1982.

75. Horton, Forest W., Jr and Donald A. Marchand, eds., *Information management in public administration*, Arlington, Virginia, Information Resources Press, 1982, 588 pp.

76. Howkins, John, Uncrossing the wires: the Hunt report in context, *Political Quarterly*, 54, 1983, 168–76.

77. Information Technology Advisory Panel, *Making a business of information: a survey of new opportunities*, London, HMSO, 1983, 53 pp.

78. *Information technology: impact on the way of life.* Proceedings of an EEC Conference on the information society, Dublin, National Board for Science and Technology, 1981, 2 vols., Conference preprints, unpaged.

79. Intergovernmental Bureau of Informatics, *IBI, informatics and the concert of nations: simultaneous growth*, Rome, IBI, 1985, 30 pp.

80. Kawahata, M., Significance of informationalisation and the basic lines of informationalisation policy, in Manten and Tinman (see no. 95), 35–57.

81. Jequier, Nicolas, Intelligence requirements and information management for developing countries, in O'Brien, Rita Cruise (see no. 108), 122–40.

82. Keren, Carl and Larry Harmon, Information service industries in less developed countries, in *Annual Review of Information Science & Technology*, ed. M.E. Williams, vol. 17, White Plains, New York, Knowledge Industry Publications, 1980, 289–324.

83. King, Donald W. et al., *Key papers in the economics of information*, White Plains, New York, Knowledge Industry Publications, 1983, 405 pp.

84. Knight, Frank, *The economics of information and uncertainty*, New York, Harper Torchbooks, 1965.

85. Kochen, Manfred, Information and society, in *Annual review of information science & technology*, ed. M.E. Williams, vol. 18, White Plains, New York, Knowledge Industry Publications, 1983, 249–80.

86. Laferriere, Daniel, Making room for semiotics, *Academe*, 65, November 1979, 434–40.

87. Library Association of Australia, ACT Branch, *Papers presented at the National Information Policy Seminar, Canberra, 7–8 December 1981*, Sydney, LALA, 1981.

88. Lloyd, Terry, To have and have not, *New Scientist*, 105, 1442, 7 February 1985, 37–38.

89. Lucas, H. C., *Introduction to computers and information systems*, New York, Macmillan, 1986, 646 pp.

90. Lytle, Richard H., IRM, 1981–86, in *Annual review of information science & technology*, ed. M.E. Williams, vol. 21, White Plains, New York, Knowledge Industry Publications, 1986, 309–36.

91. Macbride, Sean, *Many voices, one world: towards a more just and efficient world information and communication order*, New York, UNIPUB, 1980, 312 pp. (Report of the International Commission for the Study of Communication Problems.)

92. McClellan, Stephen T., Sea change in the information industry, *Datamation*, International Edition, June 1982, 88–89.

93. McIver, Robert M. and Charles H. Page, *Society: an introductory analysis*, London, Macmillan, 1947, 697 pp.

94. McLaughlin, Robert and Anthony Foley, *Information technology in Northern Ireland and the Republic of Ireland*, Belfast, Cooperation North, 1985.

95. Manten, Arie A. and Theo Tinman, eds., *Information policy and scientific research*, Amsterdam, Elsevier, 1983, 170 pp.

96. Markoski, Joseph P., Telecommunications regulations as barriers to the transborder flow of information, *Cornell International Law Journal*, 14, 1981, 287–331.

97. Matson, Floyd and Ashley Montagu, eds., *The human dialogue: perspectives on communication*, New York, Free Press, 1967, 595.

98. Melody, William H., The context of change in the information professions, *Aslib Proceedings*, 38, 8, August 1986, 223–30.

99. Melody, William H., 'The information economy: the role of public and private information', London, Polytechnic of Central London, 1985. (Annual Library Lecture.)

100. Michel, Jean, Information now: a French point of view, in Manten and Tinman (see no. 95), 129–32.

101. Mitchell, Jeremy, The information society: private monopolies and the public interest, *Political Quarterly*, 53, 1983, 160–67.

102. Naisbitt, John, *Megatrends: ten new directions transforming our lives*, New York, Warner Books, 1984, 338.

103. Narasimhan, R., The socioeconomic significance of information technology to developing countries, *The Information Society Journal*, 2, 1, 1985, 65–79.

104. *The Netherlands in the information age: a context for discussion on information policy in the Netherlands*. Prepared for the Centrum voor Informatie Beleid by Arthur D. Little, Inc. and Horringa & De Koring, The Hague, Centrum voor Informatie Beleid, 1981, 155 pp.

105. Neustadt, Richard M., Information policy: progress and prospects, *Library Journal*, 15 September 1974, 1742–46.

106. Nora, Simon and Alain Minc, *The computerisation of society: a report to the President of France*, Cambridge, Massachusetts, MIT Press, 1980, 186 pp.

107. Noyce, Robert N., Hardware prospects and limitations, in Dertouzous and Moses (see no. 37), 321–37.

108. O'Brien, Rita Cruise, ed., *Information, economics and power: the NorthGSouth dimension*, London, Hodder & Stoughton, 1983, 156 pp.

109. O'Brien, Sean, 'Information, information technology and the Third World', Masters dissertation for the Department of Information Studies, The Queen's University of Belfast, 1986, 87 pp. Unpublished.

110. Organisation for Economic Cooperation and Development, *Information activities, electronics and telecommunications technologies: impact on employment, growth and trade*, vol. 1, Paris, OECD, 1981, 136 pp.

111. Organisation for Economic Cooperation and Development, *Trends in the information economy*, Paris, OECD, 1986, 42 pp.

112. Pool, Ithiel de Sola, *Handbook of communication*, Chicago, Rand McNally, 1973, 1011 pp.

113. Porat, Marc Uri, *The information economy: definition and measurement*, 9 vols., Washington, DC, US Department of Commerce, Office of Telecommunications, 1978.

114. Rada, Juan, Information technology and the Third World, in Forester (see no. 50), 571–89.

115. Ramsey, Thomas J., Europe responds to the challenge of the new information technologies: a teleinformatics strategy for the 1980s, *Cornell International Law Journal*, 14, 1981, 237–85.

116. Reynolds, George W., *Introduction to business telecommunications*, Columbus, Ohio, Charles E. Merrill, 1984, 243 pp.

117. Robbins, Kevin, New technology: the political economy of General Ludd, in *Information technology: impact on the way of life* (see no. 78), vol. 2.

118. Rosenberg, Victor, National information policies, in *Annual review of information science & technology*, ed. M. E. Williams, vol. 17, White Plains, New York, Knowledge Industry Publications, 1982, 3–32.

119. Rubin, Michael Rogers, ed., *Information economics and policy in the United States*, Littleton, Colorado, Libraries Unlimited, 1983, 340 pp.

120. Samuelson, Paul, *Economics*, 11th edn, New York, McGraw-Hill, 1980, 838 pp.

121. Schiller, Herbert I., *Who knows: information in the age of the Fortune 500*, Norwood, New Jersey, Ablex, 1982, 187 pp.

122. Schramm, Wilbur, How communication works, in *Mass communications: selected readings for librarians*, ed. K. J. McGarry, London, Bingley, 1972, 17–38.

123. Shannon, Claude E., A mathematical theory of communication, *Bell System Technical Journal*, 27, 1948, July, 379–423, October, 656–715.

124. Smith, Anthony, Telecommunications and the fading of the industrial age, *Political Quarterly*, 54, 1983, 181–86.

125. Smith, Anthony E., The information revolution of the 1990s, *Political Quarterly*, 54, 1983, 187–91.

126. Spence, A. Michael, An economist's view of the economics of information, in *Annual review of information science & technology*, ed. Carlos Cuadra, vol. 9, White Plains, New York, Knowledge Industry Publications, 1974, 57–78.

127. Stevens, S.S., Introduction: a definition of communication, *Journal of the Acoustical Society of America*, 26, 6, 1950, 689–90.

128. Stewart, J. Allen, The Government's role: creating the right climate for the technological revolution, *Aslib Proceedings*, 36, 1, January 1984, 1–6.

129. Stonier, Tom, The microelectronic revolution: Soviet political structure and the future of East/West relations, *Political Quarterly*, 54, 1983, 137–51.

130. Stonier, Tom, *The wealth of information*, London, Thames Methuen, 1983, 24 pp.

131. Strassman, Paul A., *Information payoff: the transformation of work in the electronic age*, New York, Free Press, 1985, 285 pp.

132. Strauch, Helena M., Entrepreneurship in the information industry, in *Careers in information*, ed. Jane F. Spivack et al., White Plains, New York, Knowledge Industry Publications, 1982, 72–101.

133. Suprenant, Thomas T., Global threats to information, in *Annual review of information science & technology*, ed. M.E. Williams, vol. 20, White Plains, New York, Knowledge Industry Publications, 1985, 3–25.

134. Sutherland, Ewan, ed., Telecommunications: policy issues and regulatory practices affecting the future. Proceedings of the Salzburg Seminar, Session 243, 1985, 29 pp. Unpublished.

135. Sweet, Pat, Graphics enters the jet age, *The Observer*, 14 September 1986, 41–42.

136. Sweeney, Gerry P., Telematics and development, *The Information Society Journal*, 1, 2, 1981, 113–30.

137. Tocatlian, Jacques, National information and the General Information Programme/UNISIST, Paper presented at a Symposium held in Vienna, 5–6 April 1984. (Mittelfrigiste Perspektiven einer Informationspolitik.).

138. Tateno, Tadeo, Telecommunications administration in Japan, in Adelstein et al., op. cit.

139. Toffler, Alvin, *The Third Wave*, London, Pan, 1980, 544 pp.

140. Tracy, Michael, Telecommunications: effects on existing media, *Political Quarterly*, 54, 1983, 177–86.

141. Unesco, *First UNISIST meeting of experts on regional information policy and planning for economic and social development: a dynamic approach*. Working document for Unesco by John C. Gray, Paris, Unesco, 1977.

142. *U.K. Information Industry: current issues. Public rights of access to information*, London, British Library, 1985. (Current issues 9.)

143. Van den Brink, R., The economics of information policy, in Manten and Tinman, op. cit., 161–70.

144. Van Rosendaal, C. Jansen, European Information Policy Situation, *Aslib Proceedings*, 36, 1, January 1984, 15–24.

145. Van Trier, A.A., Knowledge industry: industry of the future, in Manten and Tinman, op. cit., 19–34.

146. Ward, Sandra, Online information: a perspective from Glaxo Research Ltd, *Aslib Information*, 14, 11/12 November/December 1986, 260.

147. Weizenbaum, Joe, The myths of artificial intelligence, in Forester, op. cit., 84–94.

148. Wellisch, Hans, From information science to informatics, *Journal of Librarianship*, 4, 3, 1972, 157–87.

149. Williams, Raymond, *Communication*, London, Chatto & Windus, 1966, 196 pp.

150. Woolston, John E., Information exchange in a North–South context, *Aslib Proceedings*, 36, 1, January 1984, 7–14.

151. Zorkoczy, Peter, *Information technology: an introduction*, New York, Van Nostrand, 1984, 140 pp.

152. Zunde, Pranas and John Gehl, Empirical foundations of information science, in *Annual review of information science & technology*, ed. M.E. Williams, vol. 14, White Plains, New York, Knowledge Industry Publications, 1979, 69–92.

153. Zurkowski, Paul G., Integrating America's Infostructure, *Journal of American Society for Information Science*, 35, 3, 1984, 170–78.

154. Zwimpfer, L.E., Communications technology: after 1984, in *Libraries: after 1984, Proceedings of the Library Association of Australia/New Zealand Library Association Conference, Brisbane, 1984*, Sydney, Library Association of Australia, 1985, 134–46.

Index